STUDIES IN PHILOSOPHY

XVI

EXPLANATION BY DESCRIPTION

AN ESSAY ON HISTORICAL METHODOLOGY

by

FRED. D. NEWMAN

Western Reserve University

1968

MOUTON

THE HAGUE · PARIS

LIBRARY OF CONGRESS CATALOG CARD NUMBER: 68-13350

Printed in The Netherlands by Mouton & Co., Printers, The Hague

To all my students and friends
and in particular
Maisie, whom I love more than I ever
believed I could love anyone

PREFACE

Not only is this book partly about *sketches*; it is itself a sketch. Initially I had intended the work to be more encyclopedic than it has turned out. One reason for abandoning this plan was the appearance of Hempel's *Aspect of Scientific Explanation*. More important, perhaps, is my belief that attempting to say something new is ultimately more justified – (though unfortunately, more pretentious) – than reviewing all that has been said. I *have*, however, tried to indicate the sources of relevant discussions.

When all is said and done I remain a Hempelian. Though I do not know them personally, the influence of Hempel, Quine and Goodman on my work is transparent. I apologize for not having done justice to these men.

I am deeply indebted to Donald Davidson, K. D. Irani, Jack Vickers, John Dolan, John Wallace, Richard Jeffrey, David Nivison and Daniel Bennett for their philosophical guidance.

My thanks to the editors of *Philosophy of Science, Theoria,* and *Ethics* for permission to reprint large portions of "Explanation Sketches", "Two Analyses of Prediction", and "The Origins of Sartre's Existentialism", which appeard first in these journals.

I wish to acknowledge the United States Air Force Office of Scientific Research (grant No. AFOSR–529-65) which covered some of the expenses incurred in the preparation of the manuscript.

I very much appreciate the help I have received from Ellen and Nancy Rozek in the typing of the manuscript.

Finally I will always be grateful to my wife Barbara Newman, my sister Pearl Cohen and my brother-in-law Lewis D. Cohen for their general encouragement.

New York City, January, 1966   F. N.

TABLE OF CONTENTS

I

INTRODUCTORY REMARKS:
IN THE BEGINNING THERE WERE THE COVERING-LAW THEORISTS

It is often said that historians *describe* what has happened rather than *explain* what has happened. And, more emphatically, that they most certainly do not *predict* what *will* happen. Frequently this is all the historian *will* say by way of characterizing the supposed methodological uniqueness of his discipline. Philosophers, and some historians, have said much more. But any philosopher who has written about historical methodology and has been concerned enough to question whether the practicing historian has any interest in his activity will probably report that most do not appear to understand the intricacies of these methodological problems. Perhaps philosophers of history should not be concerned by this. Perhaps, in fact, most aren't. It might well be that philosophers concerned with methodological problems in certain areas must learn to live with the fact that they are writing about nothing of particular interest to people participating in the discipline about which they are writing. I do not, however, believe that this need be the case. Moreover, I do not believe it should be. Therefore, I wish to examine some foundational problems of the historical discipline with the hope that this exploration will be revealing to the historian. However, I must remark that I do not intend to *water down* the analysis because of this hope. If the historian lacks the respect for his discipline that I have so much the worse for him. The methodological problems of history are intricate and require careful handling if some insight is to be gained. If understanding is to be gained no moves should be outlawed because they put too great a demand on the reader. If the historian cannot follow my discussion because it is obscure I take full responsibility. If he cannot follow because I am being *too philosophical* then it is his loss as well as mine.

Having moderately chided the historian for his lack of concern with methodological issues let me now remark that my own philosophical colleagues have been guilty of a closely related crime. Much of the contemporary literature on historical explanation as well as other topics in historical methodology has treated certain topics *in the guise of* a discussion of historical methodology. All too often discussions of historical explanation, for example, have merely been discussions of explanation. Of course it is true that historical explanations are explanations and, therefore, analyses of explanation are relevant to analyses of historical explanation. However, too frequently, the peculiar problems of historical explanation are placed in the background – quite a ways in the background. What is needed is a sensitivity to both the generality of the issue and the particularity of it. It is my hope that what follows will display that sensitivity.

It seems plain that historians explain and describe. The philosophical question concerns the sense of *description* and *explanation* employed when one speaks of explanation in history and description in history. Moreover, there are relationships between these two concepts and, thereby, between the two activities of describing and explaining. The two concepts, *explanation* and *description*, and their interrelationships are the subject matter of this essay. Put in the most general terms the thesis of the essay will be that historians frequently explain an action by offering a description of that action. It is, perhaps, a reflection of the perversity as well as the complexity of philosophy that so much can be said by way of clarifying that seemingly straightforward remark.

Good philosophical sense requires that we begin by considering a certain analysis of explanation – the so-called covering-law model. This analysis purports to serve as an analysis of one kind of explanation common to all explanatory disciplines. Proponents of the view have sometimes declared that the analysis will do as an analysis of historical explanation. It is not so much that all historical explanations are of the covering-law form. Indeed they sometimes suggest that there are explanations in disciplines other than history which do not follow the form. The claim is rather that historical explanations of the sort explicated by the covering-law analysis are no different by virtue of being historical.

The expression "covering-law theorists" – (coined by Dray) – refers to a group of philosophers almost all of whom might be said to be in the Positivist-Analytic tradition.[1] Here we shall be concerned primarily with the writings of Carl Hempel, the most important of these men.[2] In "The Logic of Explanation", Hempel and Oppenheim lay out the covering-law analysis as follows:

We divide an explanation into two major constituents, the explanandum and the explanans. By the explanandum, we understand the sentence describing the phenomenon to be explained (not the phenomenon itself); by the explanans, the class of those sentences which are adduced to account for the phenomenon. As was noted before, the explanans falls into two sub-classes; one of these contains certain sentences $C_1, C_2, \ldots, C_k$ which state specific antecedent conditions; the other is a set of sentences $L_1, L_2, \ldots, L_r$ which represent general laws.

If a proposed explanation is to be sound its constituents have to satisfy certain conditions of adequacy, which may be divided into logical and empirical conditions.[3]

In "The Function of General Laws in History", Hempel attempts

[1] Dray introduces this term to refer to such people as Hempel, Popper, and White. See William Dray, *Laws and Explanation in History* (Oxford, Oxford University Press, 1957), p. 1.

[2] The following is an incomplete list of Hempel's writings on this topic:
Carl Hempel, "The Function of General Laws in History", in *Theories of History*, Patrick Gardiner, editor (Glencoe, Ill., The Free Press, 1959), pp. 344-55.
Carl Hempel and Paul Oppenheim, "The Logic of Explanation", in *Readings in the Philosophy of Science*, Herbert Feigl and May Brodbeck, editors (New York, Appleton-Century-Crofts, Inc., 1953), pp. 319-52.
Carl Hempel, "Deductive-Nomological vs. Statistical Explanation", *Minnesota Studies in the Philosophy of Science*, Vol. III, Herbert Feigl and Grover Maxwell, editors (Minneapolis, University of Minnesota Press, 1962), pp. 98-169.
Carl Hempel, "Aspects of Scientific Explanation", in *Aspects of Scientific Explanation and other Essays in the Philosophy of Science* (New York, The Free Press, 1965), pp. 333-496.
Many of Hempel's essays are reprinted in *Aspects* including the first two mentioned above. Also in *Aspects* is a fine bibliography for this topic.

[3] Hempel and Oppenheim, *op. cit.*, p. 321.

to show that the covering-law analysis of explanation will suffice as an explication of historical explanation. In *this* work he lays out the analysis as follows:

The explanation of the occurrence of some specific kind E at a certain place and time consists, as it is usually expressed, in indicating the causes or determining factors of E. Now the assertion that a set of events – say of the kind $C_1, C_2, \ldots, C_n$ – have caused the event to be explained amounts to the statement that according to certain general laws, a set of events of the kind mentioned is regularly accompanied by an event of kind E. Thus, the scientific explanation of the event in question consists of

(1) a set of statements asserting the occurrence of certain events $C_1 \ldots C_n$ at certain times and places,

(2) a set of universal hypotheses, such that

(a) the statements of both groups are reasonably well confirmed by empirical evidence.

(b) from the two groups of statements the sentences asserting the occurrence of event E can be logically deduced.[4]

On both of these accounts explanations are construed as linguistic entities. What you explain are events. The explanation, however, is not an event. One part of the explanation is a description of the event being explained. At the very outset it must be noticed that though there is but one event being explained there are probably an infinite number of descriptions of this event. The *explanandum* is a description of the event being explained. It must, therefore, follow from the *explanans* according to the analysis. But in laying out the model Hempel has not payed sufficient attention to the fact that there are probably an infinite number of descriptions of any single event. This is, however, of considerable importance, particularly with regard to the analysis of historical explanation. Hempel speaks of "the sentences asserting the occurrence of event E". It is possible that one sentence or set of sentences asserting the occurrence of E might follow from an *explanans* X whereas another sentence or set of sentences, also asserting the occurrence of E might not. Explanations are of events under descriptions. It does not follow, of course, that explanations are of linguistic entities. It *might* follow that explanations are not unique. For an

4 Hempel, *op. cit.*, "Function", p. 345.

event E there might well be an infinite number of explanations. Notice that we have not yet committed ourselves on the question of whether these different explanations of the same event E are equivalent. This is certainly a crucial question that will receive attention. However, it is important that we first point out that there might be numerous explanations of the same event before we raise the issue of their relationships to one another.

Attacks against the covering-law model have been plentiful. In the pages that follow I shall exhibit some, though by no means all, of these objections. However, my primary aim is not to align myself completely with either Hempel or his antagonists. Rather I shall employ the Hempelian insights as well as those insights contained in objections to Hempel's position in order to further our understanding of the nature of the historical inquiry. I hasten to observe that historians do more than explain and describe. I believe, however, that explaining and describing are surely important activities engaged in by the historian. Criticizing what I have to say by pointing out that historians are people attempting to turn out imaginative prose would not be, to my mind, a reasonable criticism.

II

THE HISTORICAL EXPLANATION SKETCH

A. A TRIVIAL QUIBBLE

Though Hempel takes his analysis of explanation as a satisfactory analysis of historical explanation he does point out certain peculiarities of the historical discipline. Historians, Hempel observes, do not typically produce full blown explanations. They rather provide us with

... something that might be called an *explanation sketch*. Such a sketch consists of a more or less vague indication of the laws and initial conditions considered as relevant, and it needs "filling out" in order to turn into a full-fledged explanation. This filling out requires further empirical research, for which the sketch suggests the direction. . . .[1]

An objection to the covering-law model by way of an objection to the notion of the explanation sketch has been made by Scriven. He states this objection in the following way:

Now I have an alternative description of what Hempel calls explanation sketches. I regard them as *explanations as they stand* (italics mine), not incomplete in any sense in which they should be complete, but certainly not including the *grounds* which we should give if pressed to support them. Just as we must distinguish a statement about the population of the ancient Greek city of Poseidonis (Paestumn) from our grounds for believing it, so we must distinguish the statement of an explanation from our grounds for putting it forward as such; and amongst these grounds a further distinction is useful.[2]

[1] *Ibid.*, p. 351.
[2] Michael Scriven, "Truisms as the Grounds for Historical Explanation", in *Theories of History*, Patrick Gardiner, editor (Glencoe, Ill., The Free Press, 1959), p. 446.

I should like to consider two of the three kinds of *grounds* that Scriven distinguishes in order to point out what I take to be a serious mistake of Scriven's view. Scriven speaks of (1) truth justifying grounds; these are what we need when the truth of some assertion made in offering the explanation is questioned. He also speaks of (2) role justifying *grounds*; these are what we need when the claim that the statements made are adequate for a certain task – the task of explaining – is questioned. According to Scriven general laws should not be thought of as contained in the explanation. They are role-justifying grounds. It might be that the explanation together with its role-justifying grounds satisfy the conditions of Hempel's model. But it is surely a mistake, thinks Scriven, to lump explanations in with their justifications. Moreover, this is no small quibble. For "... once we remove from an explanation's back the burden of its own proof we are in a better position to see the criteria for judging both".[3] Despite the picturesque language I believe the quibble is small. Nonetheless I should like to begin with a brief discussion of it since its simplicity will make it easy for us to see beyond it to an important difference in attitude between covering-law theorist and reactionist which underlies this as well as *many* other less trivial quibbles. Let us, then, examine Scriven's objection.

Suppose Petula believes that the population of Nigeria is 200,000. If we were to ask her why she believed this the answer might be a justification of her belief. She might tell us that she believes it because the *World Almanac* lists the population as 200,000. But the reason that Petula believes something is not to be confused with that which she believes. Of course she must also believe that the *World Almanac* lists the populations as 200,000, but this is not the belief in question.

Suppose Herman explains why the ball fell to the floor by saying that it fell from the edge of the table. Now we ask Herman to justify his explanation. What are we asking when we ask Herman to justify his explanation? Let us consider possible forms of the questions directed to Herman. In the case of belief our question took the form (1), "Why do you believe x?" If we merely

[3] *Ibid.*

substitute "explain" for "believe" in the above question the result is (2), "Why do you explain x?" But it is apparent that if the "x" in (2) denotes that which is explained the answers most appropriate would give reasons for giving an explanation rather than reasons for giving the explanation that was given. "Why do you explain the ball's falling?" would most often be answered by such responses as, "The child was curious to know", "The teacher threatened to whip me if I didn't." This sort of paraphrasing of the belief question (1) misleads us. But this is not, perhaps, a telling argument against the analogy. What we must do is reconstruct the explanation question.

The correct paraphrasing of the belief question might be (3), "Why do you explain x by y?" or (4), "Why does y explain x?" The move from (3) to (4) is dictated by the desire to eliminate such answers as, "I believe it is correct to do so." On Scriven's anti-covering-law account what should come out as the answer to the explanation question analogous to the belief question is the general law. So then we should consider (4), viz., "Why does y explain x?" e.g., "Why does the ball's falling from the edge of the table explain its falling to the floor?" The claim is that to cite the general law at this point is sometimes appropriate. And citing the general law justifies the explanation in the same way that citing the belief about the *World Almanac* justifies the belief about the population of Nigeria. But by considering the question of form (4), it is clear that the citing of the general law would only tend to show that the ball's falling off the edge of the table *is* an explanation of its falling to the ground only if there is some general law which relates the two events. A question of form (4) is asking nothing more than (5), "Why is y an explanation of x?" And the answer "y is an explanation of x because z" (where z is a general law), hardly shows that general laws are not parts of explanations. On the contrary, it tends to show that they are.

It is of course true that z is not part of the correct analysis of explanation. But the claim is not that z or any other particular law is part of the analysis of explanation. Rather, the analysis holds that laws are parts of explanations.

Scriven's motivation, like Dray's and many others opposed

to the covering-law thesis, can be seen in the following remark:

> Explanations are practical, context bound affairs, and they are merely converted into something else when set out in full deductive array. Just as the joke becomes, when all the context is laboriously presented, a sociological explanation of a joke (and is usually no longer funny), so the explanation when dressed in its deductive robes becomes a proof or a justification of an explanation (and usually no longer explains, but demonstrates).[4]

But what does it mean to say that jokes become sociological explanations of jokes when the context is laboriously presented? Scriven takes explanations to be practical context-bound *affairs*. But it does not seem clear to me that explanations are best viewed as *affairs* at all! Perhaps it is correct to say that *explaining* is an *affair*. But there is, I believe, a useful distinction to be drawn between the activity of explaining and the concept of explanation. And it is this distinction which is invariably short-changed by those people referred to by Mandelbaum as reactionists. (Mandelbaum does not list Scriven with the "reactionists", though I fail to see why.[5]) Both covering-law theorists and reactionists *agree* that general laws rarely, if ever, *appear* in historical writings. The dispute cannot be on this point. Hempelians believe that general laws are tacitly being employed by the historian in one important phase of his activity, qua historian. To show that sometimes general laws are offered by the historian when he is asked to justify the claim that he has given a legitimate explanation is hardly to show that general laws are not covertly employed by historians when they explain. This distinction that I draw between explaining – the activity – and explanation – the concept – is one we shall confront throughout. Drawing it sharply, negating it or blurring it is common to much of the material written in this area. Hence, it is wise to stay on guard with respect to it.

---

[4] *Ibid.*, p. 450.
[5] Maurice Mandelbaum, "Historical Explanations: The Problem of 'Covering-Laws' ", *History and Theory: Studies in the Philosophy of History*, 1 (1961), pp. 229-242.

B. A NON-TRIVIAL QUIBBLE

I now wish to examine a more substantial objection to Hempel's discussion of the explanation sketch. This objection is also due to Scriven.[6]

According to Hempel in almost all cases when some historian wishes to explain why an event happened, e.g. why Washington crossed the Delaware, he offers an explanation sketch. For example, he points out that Washington wished to surprise the Hessians; that the Hessians were on the other side of the Delaware River; that the way to surprise the Hessians was to suddenly appear in their midst in the middle of the night; and so on. This remember, is a sketch offered by the historian which merely ". . . consists of a more or less vague indication of the laws and initial conditions considered as relevant".[7]

I am particularly concerned to examine what is meant by saying that the sketch gives us a ". . . more or less vague indication of the *laws* . . . considered as relevant".[8]

Scriven, we have pointed out, has suggested that what Hempel calls an explanation sketch should be described otherwise. He tries to show that what Hempel calls an explanation sketch is best viewed as an explanation as it stands, though it does not include the various *grounds* which the historian should give were he asked for a justification of his explanation. Some of these justificatory grounds would be Scriven's *role-justifying grounds* and would include general laws.

To illustrate his point, Scriven asks us to consider a proposed explanation of Cortes' third voyage. He says:

Suppose we accept the view which Merriman appears to favor in *The Rise of the Spanish Empire*: that the prospect of gigantic booty, and considerable confidence that by leading the expedition himself the previous causes of failure could be overcome were the determining factors.[9]

---

6   Scriven, *op. cit.*
7   Hempel, *op. cit.*, "Function", p. 351.
8   *Ibid.*
9   Scriven, *op. cit.*, p. 448.

Scriven holds that Merriman's account is properly construed as an explanation and contends, quite correctly, that Hempel would regard it as an explanation sketch – something less than an explanation.

Scriven argues that on the assumption that we accept Hempel's *criterion of deducibility for explanation* and his notion of an explanation sketch, the following sets of statements would complete Merriman's explanation sketch:

I.   (i)   *All confident wealth seeking people undertake any venture which offers wealth*
    (ii) *The third voyage envisioned by Cortes offered wealth*
    (iii) *Cortes was confident and wealth seeking*

II. (i)   *All confident people seeking very great wealth undertake any venture which offers very great wealth*
    (ii) *The third voyage envisioned by Cortes offered very great wealth*
    (iii) *Cortes was confident and seeking very great wealth*

III. (i)   *All confident people with Cortes' background of experience, seeking very great wealth, undertake any venture involving the hazards of this one, which offers very great wealth*
    (ii) *The third voyage envisioned by Cortes involved the hazards that it involved and offered very great wealth*
    (iii) *Cortes was confident and had Cortes' background of experience and was seeking very great wealth.*[10]

Scriven, using these three examples, offers a quasi-*reductio* of the deducibility criterion. He purports to show that either the laws in I-III are "hopelessly false" or, are trivial *truisms* (e.g., as in the case of III, covering some one phenomenon, i.e., Cortes). Therefore, I-III fail as *filling-ins*. And, says Scriven, "a moments thought" makes it clear that there is no law for a filling-in between II and III which is both true and non-trivial.

I am unhappy with the *moments thought* clause of Scriven's argument. It seems to me as if the question under consideration

10   *Ibid.*, p. 454.

should not be decided by a *moments thought* but by continuous empirical research. This matter will be discussed at some length shortly. But another feature of Scriven's argument that greatly interests me is this: The filling-ins chosen were in precisely the same terms as the original sketch. To explain why Cortes set out on his third voyage Scriven accepts Merriman's explanation. Then, he argues, if you take this explanation as a sketch the filling-in must be in the terms of the *explanandum* associated with the sketch.[11]

When Hempel says that the sketch gives a "... more or less vague indication of the laws ..." need we assume that the laws thus indicated are laws in the terms of the *explanandum* of the sketch? I think not. But Scriven's *reductio* seems to me to derive much of its force from this unstated assumption.

Mandelbaum has made this very point.[12] My argument is best taken as an application of Mandelbaum's view. Mandelbaum, speaking of explanations rather than sketches, says the following about Hempel's radiator-cracking example:

Is it the case that in order to explain this particular event, the cracking of this radiator on this particular night, there should be a law concerning the cracking of radiators; or is it sufficient in order to explain this particular event that there should be merely general laws which connect temperature and freezing, freezing and expansion, and the like?[13]

Mandelbaum answers his rhetorical question by pointing out that there need be no mention of radiators in the *explanans* of the explanation.[14] Adapting this point to my argument we should say the following: The sketch here does involve radiator talk. But this does not require our coming up with a radiator-cracking law, any more than Scriven (or Merriman) was required to search for a law

[11] I benefited greatly from discussion with Donald Davidson of Stanford University on these matters.
[12] Mandelbaum, *op. cit.*
[13] *Ibid.*, p. 232.
[14] In the actual example which appears in "The Function of General Laws in History", Hempel *does* bring in laws about temperature, expansion, etc. However, the point about redescription is not explicitly made.

in terms of Cortes-like people or wealth-seeking people, simply because the sketch was in these terms.

Given an explanation sketch – suppose we agree that there are such things – are the laws indicated by the sketch necessarily laws in terms of the *explanandum* of the sketch? Or, perhaps, more accurately, the *explanandum* for which the sketch was offered? The answer appears to me to be no. An event E_1 can be described in many different ways. Let D_1 be one of these descriptions. The historian might explain E_1 by offering a sketch in terms of D_1. To put it quite loosely, he might be thinking of E_1 as a case of Cortes taking a third voyage, or Washington crossing the Delaware, or this particular radiator cracking. But the sketch might point to filling-in laws (or justificatory grounds, if one takes Scriven's line) which are related to D_2 where D_2 is a description of the same event E_1 and where, on any intuitively acceptable criterion of equivalence, D_1 is not equivalent to D_2.

Suppose, for a brief moment, we resurrect the deducibility criterion. Then my position may be put in the following way. The laws to which an explanation sketch ES_1, together with a statement of initial conditions $i_1, \ldots, i_n$ point, may entail the event to be explained under a description D_1. But the *explanandum* associated with ES_1 need not be D_1. It is perhaps not unreasonable that Scriven should fill-in by merely forming a universal law in the terms of the *explanandum* of the sketch. Sometimes Hempel and frequently Hume, seem guilty of leading us to this view. However, reasonably interpreted, when Hempel speaks of a sketch vaguely indicating laws we may take him as merely suggesting that some laws are vaguely indicated which would make up the *explanans* of an explanation of the event in question – not necessarily in the terms which *describe* the event *in* the sketch's *explanandum*.

Now, even if we reject the entailment or deducibility condition the point still holds. The sketch might not be such that filling it in would lead to an early-Hempelian-full-blown explanation where *explanandum* is deducible from *explanans*. However, the laws "indicated" in the sketch might require a redescription of the event being explained if we are to maximize the force of the full-blown explanation – even if this full-blown explanation lacks the deducibility relationship between *explanans* and *explanandum*. For example, if we use statistical laws (as opposed to non-statistical universal laws) in our *explanans* it might often be reasonable to change the *explanandum* of the sketch (i.e., to use an alternative description of the event to be explained) in order to invoke certain of these statistical laws.

In order that *our* analysis be filled in we must establish criteria by which we can judge two descriptions, D_1 and D_2, to be descriptions of the same event E_1 and non-equivalent.

Suppose both D_1 and D_2 actually describe events. Then, taking descriptions as complete statements rather than parts of complete statements, as we have been, D_1 is equivalent to D_2 if and only if D_1 entails D_2 and conversely. To take simple cases,

(D_3) Jones didn't sit on the roof

is equivalent to

(D_4) It is not the case that Jones sat on the roof

and

(D_5) Everyone in the room was chewing tobacco

is equivalent to

(D_6) There was no one in the room who wasn't chewing tobacco.

These cases are familiar and simple because there are formal systems into which (D_3) - (D_6) can be translated and in these systems the entailment relationship is well defined and the translations of (D_3) - (D_6), *viz.* $T(D_3)$ - $T(D_6)$ are such that $T(D_3)$ entails and is entailed by $T(D_4)$ and $T(D_5)$ entails and is entailed by $T(D_6)$.[15] It is more problematical whether

(D_7) He probably ate the steak

is equivalent to

[15] It might be equally plausible to say that these formal systems exist with the well defined entailment relationship because of the intuitive obviousness of the truth of statements like "D_3 entails D_4" and "D_5 entails D_6". This, of course, smacks of Goodman's *virtuous circle*, see p. 67 of his *Fact, Fiction and Forecast*.

(D_8) He didn't necessarily eat the steak.

I shall, however, leave this criterion of equivalence of description as it stands. If the concept of *entailment* is appropriately extended then my criterion presumably is correspondingly reconstrued. Finally, D_1 is *not* equivalent to D_2 if and only if it is not the case that D_1 entails D_2 or conversely.

A description, D_2, describes the same event as a description D_1, if and only if D_2 actually describes an event, i.e. is true, and D_2 entails D_1. Hence, all equivalent descriptions describe the same event, if either description is true, but not all descriptions of the same event are equivalent. Consider the following possible *explananda:*

(A) Brutus killed Caesar
(B) Brutus stabbed Caesar to death
(C) Brutus fatally poisoned Caesar

A and B describe the same event E_1 since the event described by B occurred and B entails A. However, A does not entail B. Hence, A is not equivalent to B. C entails A. However, C does not describe the same event as A for the event described by C did not occur, i.e. C is false.[16]

---

[16] In discussion with my colleague Charles Evans it was brought out that on my criterion the following is the case: If, for example, Joe is eating fish and the book is on the table then it follows that "Joe is eating fish and the book is on the table" describes the same event as "Joe is eating fish". Also, of course, "Joe is eating fish and the book is on the table" describes the same event as "The book is on the table". However, it is obvious that "Joe is eating fish" does not describe the same event as "The book is on the table". There is a prima facie difficulty here. However, I am not yet convinced that it is a mistake to say that "Joe is eating fish and the book is on the table" describes the same event as "Joe is eating fish". To put it crudely it is not clear that a description cannot describe the same event as another description and also do something more. Or, to put it another way it is not clear that if a description D_1 describes the same event as a description D_2 and D_1 describes the same event as D_3 – where D_3 is not equivalent to D_2 – that D_2 describes the same event as D_3. However, it was plain to me before my discussion with Evans and still plainer after that more work must be done on this criterion.

I also wish to acknowledge the help given me by the referee for *Philosophy of Science* who commented on my article "Explanation Sketches", which appeared in the April, 1965 issue of that journal. He was most

The problems surrounding the proper analysis of the concept of *entailment* might leave our second criterion as suspect as the first. However, we shall so leave it.

Explanation sketches give vague indications of general laws. If we attempt to fill out the sketch leaving *explanandum* as is we *may* wind up with the kinds of difficulties pointed out by Scriven. Filling out the sketch in Scriven's manner *can* fail either because the generated laws are false or trivial. I do not believe his argument shows that they *must*. But I have been suggesting an alternative manner in which sketches indicate laws. On this account filling out the sketch may require a new *explanandum* which bears the *appropriate* relationship – whatever that may be – to the *explanandum* initially associated with the sketch.

I must also remark that in cases where filling out the sketch does consist in redescribing the *explanandum* event and then bringing in related laws, it seems to me significantly less appropriate to refer to the filling-ins as *grounds* distinct from the explanation, à la Scriven. Though he offers other arguments it seems that, in the end, it is Scriven's manner of filling in the sketch which leads him to distinguish between explanations and explanations in conjunction with their role-justifying grounds. But I shall say no more about that trivial quibble.

C. THE HISTORIAN AND THE SKETCH

The historian does explain. His explanations are *sketchy* as opposed to *full blown*. However, filling these sketches in need not consist in discovering laws and additional antecedent conditions described in terms of the concepts contained in the sketch. Are these remarks relevant to the historian because *he* is responsible for filling in the sketch? Or is the historian's responsibility merely that of offering an account which could be filled out, perhaps involving a redescription of the *explanandum* event? These two

helpful in general and the criteria of equivalence of description and sameness of event described are, in fact, his suggestions. I, of course, am responsible for them, as I have accepted and, perhaps, minutely implemented them. However, I remain greatly indebted to him for his help.

questions are most important to the historian and are exceedingly difficult to answer. There are more than two questions here for one thing. For another, as with most questions, there are numerous assumptions which have gone unstated which when brought into the open reveal implications of the many questions imbedded in the two above. Suppose we consider the second question first. Is the historian responsible for offering an explanation which is susceptible to filling out? If he is then what sorts of qualifications must the historian have? If the historian must give an account which could be turned into a full blown explanation by redescription and application of relevant laws of physics, sociology, psychology, etc. then we must assume that he would be aware of some fair amount of physics, sociology, etc. Moreover, he must have in mind, if not in hand, some criterion of equivalence of description. It need not be the one offered in Section B above, but he must have something which will do the job. This criterion will result from some kind of logical investigation. If, therefore, we place this burden on the historian, we are, indeed, expecting a great deal of him. In fact, if we ask this much of him we might go all the way and have him fill in the sketch. Thus, if we answer the second question affirmatively we might just as well answer the first question affirmatively. It is not that the historian *is* responsibile. I'm not exactly sure what sense it would make to hold him responsible. But if he is obliged to offer accounts which could be filled in then, perhaps, it would be best to let him do the actual job. The historian might be quite unhappy with this suggestion. His unhappiness would be due to the discovery that he has unexpectedly realized that he is inadequate. That is, where he once thought that doing history well involved such-and-such it now turns out to involve so-and-so. And he is not capable of handling this work. However, he might also react quite positively. After all, a great deal of responsibility has been handed the historian. He is to be, on this account, a general-scientist. He must be trained well in all explanatory disciplines in order to carry on his task. Furthermore, he must not only be the scientist he must be part analytic philosopher. Each explanation or each history book which contains explanations (which includes all of them) would come complete with a manual containing the filling-ins and, as an appendix, perhaps, a statement of the various logical criteria necessary for employing the filling-ins in the manual. If we were to accept this view we should be adopting in part the attitude of strongly committed positivistic covering-law theorists. And we should be dramatically disregarding the reactionistic, common sense position which asks us to focus much more on what the historian actually does. I think that raising the questions as we have and making the bold suggestion above is exceedingly helpful in getting straight on the real *practical* issue implicit in the dispute between covering-law and non-covering-law theorists. Reactionists report that historians explain quite well without employing laws. Covering-law theorists agree that laws are not employed in the sense that they are articulated. With the problem thus stated we are hard pressed to know how to go on. But if we boldly recommend a change in the historical enterprise of the sort we have been considering then we may be able to see what is entailed by this recommendation. It is in this spirit that the above recommendation is made.

The historian could respond to the above suggestion by asking why he might not develop his own laws. After all, he might say, as long as I was able to get on without laws who needed historical laws? But since I'm burdened with filling in my own explanations why shouldn't I generate historical laws which will serve in my filling-ins? In fact the shrewd historian, willing to go along with the program outlined above, might see that if he can develop his own laws he can eliminate from his manual the appendix including the criterion of equivalence of description. Edgar Zilsel, in his article "Physics and the Problems of Historico-sociological Laws", appears to assume such a posture.[17] The general theme of Zilsel's article is that history is not to be thought of as being without laws – its own laws – and the reason it often is has to do with certain illegitimate comparisons that are commonly made between history and physics. Let us enumerate these.

---

[17]   Edgar Zilsel, "Physics and the Problem of Historico-Sociological Laws", in *Readings in the Philosophy of Science*, Herbert Feigl and May Brodbeck, editors (New York, Appleton-Century-Crofts, Inc., 1953), pp. 714-22.

(1) The investigation of laws in history has barely begun, Zilsel claims. Construction of theories from which laws are deducible (as is the case with physics) would serve only to impair empirical research and, therefore, the finding of empirical laws. But since there is no basic difference between isolated empirical laws and laws that are deduced or deducible from a more general theory, we need not be concerned about this difference.

(2) Many physical laws are discovered in laboratories. Thus, isolated systems can be created which eliminate undesirable interference. History should be compared with geophysics rather than with laboratory physics.

(3) It is difficult to ascertain the basic elements in terms of which the laws are to be formulated. That is, since generals have a greater influence on a society $Z - (Z =$ the Army) – then do privates, it should be obvious that we cannot have a law such as "Whenever the overwhelming majority of people in S want y, then . . .", which overlooks the difference between generals and privates in Z.

Zilsel goes on to offer some examples of historical laws. We shall consider an abbreviated list:

(a) Individualized art and poetry are preceded by anonymous folk art and poetry; signed paintings and sculptures by non-signed work.

(b) Free artists, such as sculptors, painters, and architects, gradually develop from craftsmen, such as stone dressers, whitewashers, and masons.

(c) Biased hero-worship precedes impartial genius-worship.

(d) If under favorable circumstances a past culture is revived after centuries, the imitators and bearers of this intellectual movement are characterized by the following traits: They do not belong to the clergy; they are scribes and secretaries in political services and develop under favorable circumstances to free literati; they are exceedingly proud of their ability to write and read and thus disdain the illiterate; they believe that the educated man is chiefly distinguished by perfection of his literary style.

It is wrong, says Zilsel, to scoff at these laws by uttering the true-but-trivialism "History never repeats itself". Physics doesn't either. These laws, or candidates for laws, present tremendous problems, especially with regard to their verification or confirmation. However, it is clear that Zilsel is willing to take his chances on them, for he claims that they, like all laws, must stand or fall on the basis of predictions or retrodictions made by employing them. Finally, Zilsel makes the following obscure point: There might well be certain of these historical laws which do not "become psychologically evident". The obscurity is due to the fact that two points are being made here of different degrees of interest. One point is that it should not count against a law L which is constructed in terms of groups that it is not psychologically evident why, e.g. masons, should want to become artisans. The second point, and I believe the more important one, is that it should not be assumed that explanations of group behavior must necessarily be reducible to explanations of the behavior of individuals who comprise the group.

The proposed laws (a), (b), (c) and (d) are certainly wanting in many respects. Zilsel is the first to concede this, and attributes it to the fact that comparative history is in its infancy. There is, however, the uncomfortable feeling that Zilsel has "fallen into the Humean trap". This involves giving in to the temptation to explain radiator failures by laws which are constructed in terms of radiators. I suspect that there is a serious mistake in believing that these types of laws are the ones which must appear in full-blown explanations of historical events. Would Hempel say that an explanation using a law such as (a), (b), (c) or (d) is merely an explanation sketch which needs filling out? And in what would the filling-out consist? Two alternatives seem to present themselves. Let us call them "filling out the sketch₁" and "filling out the sketch₂", abbreviated F.O.S.$_1$ and F.O.S.$_2$. F.O.S.$_1$ involves filling out the sketch which made use of either (a), (b), (c) or (d) in such a way as to *decrease* the generality of the law. The laws, as they stand, seem false. But they do serve to "show us the way". We must tighten up the laws by making them more specific, by having them more intimately connected with the event they are serving to explain. A possible difficulty here has been pointed out by Scriven. F.O.S.$_1$ might fail because the end product of this method is not a law, since it might cover only the one case which it purports to explain. On the other hand, this is not *necessarily* the case. At any rate Scriven surely does not show it to be. F.O.S.$_1$, therefore, *need* not fail. We must, however, recognize that it may. F.O.S.$_2$ involves *increasing* the generality of the explanation by (1), breaking down the complex event into smaller parts and (2), invoking more general laws to cover the new description of the event which resulted from (1).

To claim that either F.O.S.$_1$ or F.O.S.$_2$ is *the* correct historical procedure would be, in effect, to affirm or deny a reductionistic thesis a priori. And I agree with Zilsel and Mandelbaum that this would be a mistake. My alternative is to affirm both. It has frequently been remarked that there is no decision procedure which determines, in general, whether, given a piece of apparently disconfirming evidence e with respect to some law L, we reject the law L or reject the seeming evidence e. Analogously, I hold, there is no decision procedure for determining whether F.O.S.$_1$ or F.O.S.$_2$ is the appropriate method to be employed, given some explanation sketch. Lacking a decision procedure this matter must be left to the judgment of the historian.

Many would take the radical reductionistic position that the sketch should always be filled out by redescribing and then looking for the laws in other disciplines. On this view, history is an essentially derivative science.[18] The laws which make the explanations of the historian work are physical or psychological or sociological and thus history is, in some sense, reducible to these disciplines. All our talk about redescription of the explanandum event would seem to hint that such a reductionistic view is being endorsed. However, I by no means wish to endorse such an attitude. I see no a priori argument which establishes it. Indeed, I have agreed that F.O.S.$_2$ might be appropriate for any given sketch. Moreover, it might be the move for every sketch. But this cannot be established a priori. Historians have the option of turning to existing laws of other disciplines in which case they might be obliged to redescribe the event being explained or seeking out

---

[18] See for example, Morton White, "Historical Explanation", *Mind*, 52 (1943), pp. 212-29.

laws in terms of the concepts involved in their sketch. A third alternative quite naturally suggests itself. Mightn't the historian search for laws which will alter his description but which happen to be laws of no other discipline? I believe he may do so. It should be apparent that my attitude on these matters is rather liberal! I see no point in saying that the historian, qua historian, may not fill out the sketch. If you persist in claiming that when he does so he is acting as a sociologist or a physicist or what have you I believe you must first of all account for those cases where his filling-ins are not accomplished by employing sociological or physical laws. But more importantly would you wish to hold tenaciously to the view that when the ordinary man appeals to a law of physics in filling in an ordinary language explanation he is then explaining, qua physicist? My objection is not to the effect that you can't say this but rather why bother? The situation with the historian seems very much the same to me. The program outlined above does not show history to be something less than a bonafide science. It will sometimes employ the results of other sciences but this would not seem to distinguish it. Moreover, there is no way of showing, I claim, that the historian must turn to other disciplines for his laws. I have attempted to show some relationships between explaining and describing. The historian sometimes explains by describing in the sense that he frequently must redescribe in order to explain. This, of course, is not unique to history. However, I believe it would be a more common procedure in history than in many other sciences simply because of the distinct lack of historical laws. It must be remembered that the suggestion I am making is that the historian *should* be *prepared* to fill in his own sketches. It is surely not that he now does. Also, it is not that he must, in fact, fill in all sketches. Matters of style and such might make imprudent the attempt to fill in all those sketches which could be filled in. It is no more incumbent upon the historian to *actually* fill in all his sketches than it is incumbent upon the physicist to fill in all his or, for that matter, upon the mathematician to fill in all his proofs. What is the case is the following: Insofar as the historian fails to fill in he has less than a totally satisfactory explanatory account. Some might hold that the historian could offer explanations without the ability to fill them in. He could have some idea as to the laws that would be employed were he to fill them in but need not be in a position to offer the detailed account. He is, it might be thought, much like the reasonably sophisticated ordinary man who offers explanations to his children by alluding to laws of physics but is not able to do all the physics required to give the complete answer. With these remarks I should agree. However, it seems plain that the ordinary man who can fill in in the greatest detail is the ordinary man who is offering the better explanation. Here, of course, I do not mean the more satisfying to the questioner. After all the questioner might be satisfied without the explainer having to go very far at all. Going further than is necessary in the presentation of an explanation is like over-selling a pair of galoshes. The results might be pragmatically disastrous – both the customer and the questioner might be dissatisfied. However, there is surely a sense in which the ordinary man in a position to *go all the way* is a better explainer than the ordinary man who cannot. Such is the case with the historian.

Many in the positivistic tradition view history as something other than a real science. They are of the opinion that history is "really" sociology or some other supposed scientific discipline.[19] Though I accept a great deal of the positivistic attitude, I obviously do not share this view. One can surely be a committed covering-law theorist without adopting this attitude. And though my form of the covering-law position is not incompatible with the *history-isn't-a science* position it is even less likely that someone would hold to it while rejecting the claim that history is a science. Indeed, on my view, history is something of a *superscience*.

But even those who are anxious to endorse what I have said so far would be reluctant to think that I have painted the whole picture. They should be right. There are other dimensions of the historical activity that we have not looked at as yet which are plainly related to explaining. Interestingly enough the considerations that follow will show the historian to be even more of the *super-scientist* than those that preceded.

[19] *Ibid.*

III

FROM CATERPILLAR TO BUTTERFLY:
A CASE HISTORY OF THE HOW-POSSIBLY *

I have come to the position that the remarks that follow might well be looked upon as a short history of a brief statement on a small point in contemporary philosophy of history. An idea was presented in 1957 which has been reacted to since by a handful of people in articles, at meetings, and in personal conversation.[1] Even though progress is not philosophy's *most* important product, one should be a little disturbed by the lack of movement on this question. Maybe I have come to view these remarks as chronicle-

---

* See John Kemeny, *A Philosopher Looks At Science* (New York, Van Nostrand, 1959), p. ix.

[1] I am very grateful to Professor William Dray for the time he has given in discussion and correspondence. Though the view under attack is his, he has always been patient and sympathetic in considering rejoinders and reconstructions. He is in no way responsible for any mistakes that appear here though it is, in part, his *mistakes* that are discussed. But I must acknowledge his help, particularly since it has always emerged from an interest in clearing up the issue. The following is a partial listing of the relevant literature:

W. Dray, "Explanatory Narrative in History", *Philosophical Quarterly*, January, 1954.

W. Dray, *Laws and Explanation in History* (Oxford, 1957).

W. Dray, "More On Explaining How-Possibly" (unpublished).

P. H. Nowell-Smith, Review, *Philosophy*, April, 1959.

J. Passmore, "Laws and Explanation in History", *Australian Journal of Politics and History*, November, 1958.

J. Pitt, "Generalizations in Historical Explanation", *Journal of Philosophy*, 1959, pp. 581-3.

P. F. Strawson, Review, *Mind*, April, 1959.

I have also been helped by discussion on these matters with Professor Jaegwon Kim of Brown University, Professors Donald Davidson and David Nivison of Stanford University, and Professor Daniel Bennett of Brandeis University.

like because of a feeling that a critical history could put an end to the particular issue and, more importantly, reveal the interesting and crucial questions which underlie and the thesis that emerges from the dispute.

In the final chapter of his book *Laws and Explanation in History*, William Dray attempts to depict a type of explanation which he believes to be radically different from the type of explanation which is the concern of Hempel and other covering-law theorists.[2] The covering-law theorist is anxious to deal with explanations which emerge as typical responses to questions of the form, "Why did E Happen?" – where E is some event. Dray points out that explanations sometimes emerge as typical responses to questions of the form, "How is it possible that E happened?" The explanations which come forward as answers to how-possible questions are, on Dray's view, *bona fide* explanations. However, the analysis of this kind of explanation shows it to be structurally different than that kind of explanation which typically emerges as an answer to a why question. Hence, the covering-law analysis is, at best, a correct explication of only one kind of explanation.

Dray's position might be summarized in the following way: Consider a set G of general laws $L_1 \ldots L_n$ which *cover* events $E_1 \ldots E_n$. We may explain an event E_k in one of two ways – we may show why it happened or we may show how it was possible that it happened. It is clear, thinks Dray, that when one gives an explanation of the how-possibly type no use need be made of any L_i which is a member of the set G. To be sure the event being explained is covered by some L_i. But no L_i plays a role in the how-possibly sort of explanation. More accurately, if employed it does not play the same role as it does or would in a why explanation of the same event. *Deductiveness* is not the essential characteristic of how-possibly explanations. Therefore, general laws, which are used to obtain deductiveness in why explanations, are not employed in how-possibly explanations. At any rate, they are not employed to this end.

Dray offers a number of examples in his attempt to elucidate the notion of explanation how-possibly. He displays a variety of

[2] See, for example, the literature mentioned in footnote 2 on p. 13.

situations which are such that a confrontation of them by an agent invariably leads to a peculiar sort of puzzlement. This puzzlement is manifest in the agent's typical verbal response to the confrontation of the situation. He asks how the situation is possible – how the happening could possibly have happened. It must not be thought that Dray sees himself as attempting to analyze how-possibly explanations in terms of the typical reactions of agents to certain sorts of situations. It is, indeed, tempting to think so on the basis of Dray's final chapter as well as other comments he has made on the matter. However, he has explicitly denied this charge. Rather, he wishes to be taken as merely *pointing out* the kind of explanation he intends to analyze by suggesting these situations which provoke the puzzlement manifest in the how-possible question. Having thus drawn our attention to this kind of explanation he purports to show that its logical structure is different than that of the explanation why. Dray has made it clear in conversation, if not in his writings, that he is no more anxious to analyze how-possibly explanation in terms of psychological reactions than Hempel is to analyze why explanations in terms of psychological reactions.

Let us turn, then, to the most popular of these situations depicted by Dray.

S_1: We are radio listeners familiar with the ball park from which a ball game is being broadcast. The announcer who, we have reason to believe, is an accurate announcer, reports that a ball has been caught at the top of the center field fence. We know that the fence in question is twenty feet high.[3]

Confronted with S_1 we are perplexed and have need of an explanation. Dray's view is that the event in question – the catching of the ball – is explained when it is pointed out that there was a platform at the rear of the center field wall. Pointing out that there was a platform does not, however, explain *why* the center-fielder caught the ball. Furthermore, it does not explain *how* he caught it. Rather, it explains how he *could* have caught it.

On virtually any analysis of prediction the reaction to Dray's final chapter by a philosopher even moderately moved by the

3   Dray, *Laws, op. cit.,* p. 164.

covering-law position is easily predictable. For one thing, though Dray *has* explicitly denied that he is attempting to characterize explanation how-possibly in psychological terms, he can hardly deny that he is characterizing explanation how-possibly in terms of the use(s) to which they are put. He remarks that,

... The essential feature of explaining how-possibly is thus not that it is given of happenings which cannot be brought under a law. It is rather that it is given in the face of a certain sort of puzzlement.[4]

He also says that,

... the explanation [how-possibly] consists in showing that in spite of appearances to the contrary, it [the occurrence] is not an impossible one after all.[5]

And he says of explaining how-possibly and explaining why-necessarily that they,

... are logically independent in the sense that they have different tasks to perform.[6]

Those of us who are quick to invoke the meaning-use distinction can be expected to see Dray as confusing the activity – explaining – with explanation – the concept. Of course, Dray would hardly see it as a confusion. But there is a second reaction, perhaps somewhat less predictable, which leads, I believe, to some interesting developments. Since developments have been noticeably lacking in this area it is worth looking at this reaction. Consider then, the following reaction to Dray's remark about S_1:

First of all, why are we perplexed? Isn't it because we have good reason to believe that the following covering-law is sound: Human beings, center fielders or otherwise, cannot jump twenty feet in the air? If we were not aware of this there would be no problem at all. This can be seen by considering that a Martian, newly arrived from Mars, and as yet unfamiliar with the restriction placed on humans by our particular gravitational field, would not find S_1 at all surprising. (Assume that he had been a regular

---

4   *Ibid.*, p. 165.
5   *Ibid.*, p. 161.
6   *Ibid.*, p. 162.

listener of ball games in his rocket ship but had not noticed that there had been no cases of balls being caught twenty feet off the ground. Given that most radio announcers do not believe Martians to be in their listening audience, this assumption is not unlikely.) Now Dray's suggestion is that we can explain the situation to a fellow human being by merely pointing out the fact that there was a platform by the center field wall which the center fielder employed. Dray suggests that to cite a covering-law would be inappropriate. Consider, however, that the explanation of the how-possibly type that Dray offers only makes sense in *his* terms – that is, only serves to *eliminate puzzlement* – if there is some covering-law or connecting principle – e.g., something of this sort: With the assistance of a twenty-foot ladder leading up to a platform, people find it possible to attain heights of twenty-odd feet and simultaneously catch fly balls. For if the person who was offered this how-possibly explanation was not aware of this covering-law the explanation how-possibly would plainly not resolve his puzzlement.

Passmore has reacted in a manner not at all unlike the one just depicted.[7] He has remarked that the explanation of the catch should be seen to have the familiar covering-law pattern. Its form is as follows: A professional outfielder on a platform can catch a high ball; this professional outfielder was on a platform; therefore, he can catch the ball.

Both of these accounts amount to putting the explanation how-possibly into the covering-law form and, thereby, retaining *deductiveness* as an essential feature of explanation. Dray, commenting on Passmore's position, concedes that,

... the validity of the reasoning he sets out is indeed assumed by the how-possibly explanations we are considering: it is a condition of its acceptability.[8]

However, Dray does not agree that this shows how-possibly explanation to be of the same type as why-necessarily explanation. The difficulty, as Dray conceives it, is that putting how-possibilies into their deductive form results in an explanandum which is a

[7] Passmore, *op. cit.*, pp. 272-3.
[8] Dray, "More", *op. cit.*

possibility of an event as opposed to a description of the event. Therefore, you obtain the *deductiveness* at the expense of another necessary condition of Hempelian explanations, *viz.* that the *event* is explained – a description of the *event* is deduced.

The counter objection to this counter objection by Dray in also quite predictable. And, it brings us closer to the heart of the issue. This objection comes to the following: If you wish to view Dray's explanation how-possibly as an explanation at all it must be seen as an explanation of the possibility of an occurrence rather than a structurally different type of explanation of the occurrence. Thus, an extreme covering-law sympathizer might see the explanation how-possibly as an essentially standard explanation of a possible event. Dray sees how-possblies as a different kind of explanation of the event.

In conversation with Professor Dray I had noticed that at precisely this point in the dispute things seemed to bog down dramatically. In his unpublished comments Dray directs himself to this point.

Against the covering-law attitude – it really is seen by many reactionists as more of an attitude than a position – Dray urges two considerations. Dray concedes that the first will not appeal very much to convinced covering-law theorists. This objection is that taking the hard deductivist line leaves the deductivist with an almost purely stipulative explication. They should have failed to explicate an existing notion of explanation. Dray is surely right in saying that this will not appeal to convinced covering-law theorists. However, it is Dray's second consideration that I am most interested in commenting on. Dray says that,

... the argument used to deny that the alleged how-possibly explanation explains the *catch* can surely be turned against all those *inductive* versions of the covering-law model which Hempel himself has been the first to welcome and elaborate. If we can explain only what we can deduce strictly, then any so called inductive explanation of a given occurrence will turn out not to be an explanation of *it* either – but only of its probability.[9]

This argument seems strange in many ways. For one thing, on

9   *Ibid.*

the covering-law thesis we do not explain what we deduce, we explain by virtue of a deduction. Even if you regard the deduction as a deduction of a probability statement it is the event that is explained by the deduction – not the probability statement. But let me ignore this point and rather grant that explanations-why with statistical general laws are explanations, in the deductive sense, only of probabilities of events and not of events. Having thus granted this point we may now examine deductive how-possiblies and deductive why-probablies. I am suggesting, in effect, that Dray is willing to have us regard how-possiblies as deductive explanations of possibilities provided that we are willing to regard why explanations as deductive explanations of probabilities. Having agreed to, let us compare and contrast the two notions.

Dray reports on an observation made by Paul McEvoy.[10] Mr. McEvoy has remarked that there may have been actual states of affairs which, if known about, could have dissolved the agent's puzzlement but which, in fact, had nothing to do with the occurrence of the event in question. Suppose, for example, that the center fielder actually wore anti-gravity shoes which he *could* have employed to elevate himself twenty feet off the ground. However, he didn't. He climbed the ladder up to the platform instead. Pointing out that the center fielder wore anti-gravity shoes could have satisfied the bewildered agent. But it would be, I should think, less satisfactory to us if not to him. This is so not because one state of affairs is actual and the other possible. Both were the case. But in establishing a criterion of relevance for how-possiblies Dray would be obliged, I think, to turn how-possiblies into what McEvoy has called how-actualies. In doing so, however, he would turn how-possiblies into explanations how. Explanations how are, roughly, detailed tracing of the steps which led to a certain occurrence. They do not differ radically from explanations why. Dray has remarked elsewhere that how-possiblies are no more explanations how than they are explanations why. But to resolve McEvoy's puzzle they would have to be turned into explanations how which are, on my view, *bona fide* explanations.

Pitt has also objected that Dray has need of a criterion of relevance.[11] Dray, in countering this claim, remarks that, ". . . such relevance is established by our recognizing the explanatory facts as rebutting the conclusion", "The catch was impossible . . ."[12] And then, ". . . they (the particular facts) rebute the *specific* presumption of impossibility that arose in this particular case . . .".[13] Dray considers as other possible puzzle resolving candidates such things as the weather over Australia. Certainly the relevance criterion must distinguish between the weather over Australia and the fact that the center fielder wore anti-gravity shoes. Dray has not offered a criterion of relevance at all unless it be one in terms of psychological reactions which he claims he is not willing to do and which he surely hasn't done in any complete way.

The information in the *explanans* of why-probablies as well as how-actualies must justifiably tend to increase our degree of belief that the event in question occurred. And this is mirrored in the probability value in the *explanandum*. *New* information in the *explanans* of a why-probably or a how-actually likewise must justifiably increase our degree of belief that the event occurred and, therefore, the probability value in the *explanandum* goes up. But pure how-possiblies do not have this feature. A necessary condition of an explanation of an event is that what is offered by way of explanation justifiably increases our degree of belief that the event occurred and that the *explanans* be susceptible to filling in which will further increase our degree of belief that the event being explained occurred. How-possiblies only do this if we turn them into how-actualies. However, then they become very much like why-probablies. How-possiblies *lack* the essential feature of explanation. Even when we agree to take explanations why-necessarily as explanations why-probably they *have* it.[14]

Let me summarize this argument. I believe Dray can offer no good reason for having us call how-possiblies explanations of events rather than explanations of possible events. If he insists

[11] Pitt, *op. cit.*, pp. 581-3.
[12] Dray, "More", *op. cit.*
[13] *Ibid.*
[14] This should bring to mind Hempel's *condition of adequacy* as discussed, for example, in "Aspects", pp. 367-8. Considerable discussion of the condition will be presented in this essay.

that we thereby commit ourselves to regarding standard scientific explanations as explanations of probable events we can still counter by pointing out that even so construed these explanations are such than an *explanans* of such an explanation justifiably increases our belief in the *explanandum*-event and is susceptible to further filling in. But how-possiblies so construed lack this characteristic. The likely modifications to overcome this difficulty would turn how-possiblies into genuine explanations – things covering-law theorists would accept as explanations of events.

When we are informed that the center fielder wore anti-gravity shoes our degree of belief that the event occurred is, more than likely, increased. But are we justified in assigning a higher probability to the event? His anti-gravity shoes had nothing to do with the catch. When we get the information that there was a platform with a ladder we may justifiably increase our degree of belief that the event occurred. But why? Because he climbed the platform to get the ball. But now we are offering a how-actually, which is like a how, which is like a why in the crucial respects.

It is not the case that we do not believe an event E_1 occurred when we offer an explanation. Quite the opposite. We do believe the event occurred when we ask for an explanation. An essential feature of the explanation of this event, however, is that our degree of belief that the event occurred increases as we fill in the explanation sketch. This, I suggest, is really the essential feature of the covering-law views. But how-possiblies do not have this essential feature. On the contrary, they are given to rebut the presumption that an event couldn't have occurred. But once given they cannot increase the probability that the event did occur. They are not susceptible to filling in. No new information can be added to how-possiblies to increase the probability that the event occurred. Ironically, they bear a strong resemblance to formal proofs and are not properly regarded as explanations.

What Dray calls an explanation how-possibly is best construed as a piece of information which often makes explanations possible. The information is a pre-requisite for explanation. However, it is not itself an explanation. It can, however, be an important part of the explanatory process. We shall consider this shortly.

Dray has agreed that the *explanans* of the pure how-possibly does not offer evidence that the event in question occurred whereas the explanans of the why-probably does.[15] But it has been pointed out that one need not, perhaps, one ought not grant this.[16] It has been said that if by "justifiably increase of degree of belief" we mean something like what Carnap means, then:

(1) We ought not distinguish between the centerfielder wearing the anti-gravity shoes and the ladder against the platform even though he used the ladder.

and

(2) That there was a ladder against the platform does justifiably increase our degree of belief that the ball was caught. But, by (1) so does the fact that the centerfielder wore anti-gravity shoes.

The defense of this position is two-pronged. Oddly enough the two groups defending this manner of resurrecting the how-possibly are ordinary language types on the one hand and formalists on the other. The ordinary language approach goes something like this:

In typical why explanations the recipient of the explanation is already convinced that the event occurred. Hence, it seems unreasonable to say that the explanation increase his belief that the event occurred. Of this he had no doubt at the outset. Quite the contrary with the how-possibly. It is the paradigm case of explanation increasing degree of belief that an event occurred. Hence, if this characteristic rather than absolute deductiveness is the essential characteristic, how-possiblies display it more conspicuously than any other kind of explanation.

The formalist approach focuses on (1) and goes something like this:

The relationship between evidence and hypothesis is logical.

[15] Dray has commented on these matters while remarking on an earlier version of this essay.

[16] Some of the remarks that follow were stimulated by a discussion of a paper on this topic which I delivered at Michigan State University. I am particularly indebted to Professor G. Massey of Michigan State University for his helpful criticism. Also I wish to thank Professor Martin Lean of Brooklyn College of the City University of New York for making a correction in the statement of the Carnapian criticism of my anti-how-possibly position.

There is a logical relationship which holds between a set of evidence statements S_1 containing "The centerfielder wore anti-gravity shoes" (e_1), and "The centerfielder caught the ball at the top of the twenty foot high center field fence" (h_1). This relationship holds whether e_1 is true or false. There is, likewise, a logical relationship between a set of evidence statements S_2 containing "There was a platform with a ladder against it by the centerfield wall" (e_2) and h_1. What probability is assigned to h_1 is a function of the evidence. But the assignment is independent of whether or not the evidence statement e_n is true or false. The probability assignment to h_1 on S_1 might be equal to the probability assignment to h_1 on S_2. In fact, it might be higher. And this probability assignment indicates how rational it is to believe h_1 on the supposition that the members of S_n hold. But it is not a function of whether or not e_n which is a member of S_n holds. It is true that a set of evidence statements S_3 containing "The centerfielder wore anti-gravity shoes but did not use them" (e_3), being a different set of evidence statements, might bear a different logical relationship to h_1. But again, this is not a function of the truth or falsity of e_3. This objection is interesting. Indeed, I am struck by the claim that the *gravity-shoe* story might increase our belief more than the platform-ladder. It makes me more suspicious than ever of Carnapian probability theory. But I need not carry this any further since this objection does not tell against my point as it stands. The most that has been shown is that the how-possibly justifiably increases our degree of belief that the event being explained took place. However, the condition I have imposed is a conjunction, *viz.* that the explanation must justifiably increase our degree of belief *and* that it be such that more information can be obtained which would justifiably increase our degree of belief still further. The how-possibly fails to satisfy the condition laid down by this second conjunct so long as it remains a how-possibly. Hence, I still should contend that how-possiblies are not genuine explanations.

IV

HOW POSSIBLIES, HOW ACTUALIES
AND HOW HISTORIANS EXPLAIN

If I am right there are problems raised in Chapter III for the inductive logician. Having burdened the historian with a great deal I shall leave him out of these matters. However, in the course of our discussion of the how-possibly a number of significant developments took place which are of great interest to both philosopher of history and historian. Three developments are of the greatest interests. They are:

D (1) the essential feature of historical explanation – (if not all explanation) – is not deductiveness but rather (a) that explanations justifiably increase degree of belief that the event being explained occurred, and (b) that they be such that more information will justifiably increase our degree of belief that the event occurred.

D (2) there is an activity called "explaining how something or another is possible" which is engaged in by the historian though perhaps it is not best characterized as explaining.

D (3) there is an activity called "explaining how something or another actually happened" which is engaged in by historians and is, indeed, best characterized as explaining.

Let us first consider D (3). Some would hold that explaining how something or another happened is the paradigm of historical explanation. Explaining how something happened is rather like describing in detail the chain of events that led from something C to something else H. One might view explaining how as in some way analogous to instructions for building a model dinosaur. There we have quasi-imperatives which issue commands to be followed in a definite sequence the result of which is the constructed model dinosaur. Suppose we have as the final step (n) "Pick up completed dinosaur and admire!" Then the whole set of instructions, (1)-(n), is analogous to the explanation how which would have as its nth step, e.g. "And that's how Corte's came to take a third voyage." Explaining how amounts to tracing the detailed steps which resulted in the event under consideration. Explaining how something happened is describing how that something happened. Here, and in the case of explaining what happened, we seem to have cases where describing is more than a part of the explanatory process; it *is* the explanation. The practicing historian might well take this as a much fairer way of depicting his explanatory method. Much has been said on these matters in the philosophical literature.[1] The reactionists, as we might expect, focus quite a bit on explaining how and explaining what since they view it as true to what is really going on in history much of the time. The covering-law theorist tends to hold that these 'types' of explanations are merely poorly disguised standard-type explanations of the covering-law form.[2] Explanations how tacitly assume general statements as much as explanations why. All that is happening is that more laws need be implicitly invoked since a more detailed account is being offered. So if you explain D by pointing out that A led to B and B led to C and C led to D then you must fill in by showing how A led to B, etc. In fact, on our modified version of the Hempelian model explaining how is easily understood as spelling out in more detail in order that the laws governing the relationships which ultimately lead to the event being explained should be more evident. However, there does seem to be a point to the reactionists drive to draw a distinction between explanation why and explanation how.

Suppose little Timothy has managed to make a blond of his two-year old sister by pouring peroxide over her head. Mother comes home and asks Timothy to explain how it happened. Tim hasn't the vaguest idea but he is able to roughly trace the steps

[1] For example, much of Dray's work on the problem of historical explanation.
[2] Hempel, *op. cit.*, "Function".

which led to the result. He is telling mother what happened. Of course, it must be noticed that even our bewildered Tim does not mention that he had stolen three pieces of double bubble from the candy story the day before. He has some vague idea of what to include and what to leave out. It is not plain that he is explaining how little sister's hair got to be yellowish. On the other hand, it isn't plain that he isn't. It is in this sense that some would say historians explain. They tell us what happened. Indeed, they, like Timmy, know that certain things must be left out. But also like Timmy, they have no idea what the causal factors were which led from the pouring to the change of color. The historian tells us what has gone on. He describes the past. But he does not explain what he describes except insofar as the describing is explaining. One might almost say that this point of view takes the historian to be engaged in an activity not unlike the scientist, qua gatherer of information. The scientist must first get the facts before he can account for them. The historian, on the view being put forth, is primarily an information gatherer. History books are reports of the historians' findings. Contained are descriptions of what he has found to be the case. As I have said when talking about young Tim the historian displays some sensitivity to what is relevant to his particular purpose and what is not. That is, he knows roughly what to bring in when describing the French Revolution, the Civil War, etc. The covering-law theorist is quick to point out that precisely *this* ability to discriminate reveals the fact that the historian is tacitly employing general laws. And, indeed, he is right. However, there still appears to be some force left to the historian's claim that his main concern is to get down what happened and how it happened rather than explaining why what happened happened. Viewing the historian this way makes him a sort of pre-scientist rather than a super-scientist. He, in a sense, supplies the facts that much be accounted for by scientific disciplines. This is not to say that the historian is actually in the employ of the scientist. Most often the scientist gets his own information using certain devices, actual and conceptual, which the historian does not employ. However, the historian is a pre-scientist in this sense. He is describing, in ordinary terms and without conceptual scientific tools, what goes on. His lack of conceptual tools in not a shortcoming of his discipline. Rather, it reveals a significant difference between *his* discipline and a *true* scientific discipline. Science must have something to explain in order to be operative. The world provides for this. However, it is also true that things must be characterized in pre-scientific terms before science can account for these happenings, thus delineated, in scientific terms. This is what the historian is doing. More correctly, this is the sort of thing the historian is doing. I confess this line of thought has an appeal. However, it surely does not show that the historian is not *likewise* properly concerned with explaining in the sense of explaining why things happen. For as I have remarked the scientist both gathers his information and explains. Similarly the historian can gather his information and also explain. What *is* important to notice here is that there is an intimate relationship between the gathering process and the explanatory process.[3] What information you gather depends, in part, on what you wish to explain. On the other hand what you want to explain is determined, in part, by what information you gather. We should see then that the historian, like all other scientists, is both gathering and explaining. Is the historian in an unusual position in the sense that he *must* employ ordinary language because *someone* must do so in order that there be explanatory disciplines at all? I think not. For there is no clear cut line between ordinary language and scientific language, anymore than there is a clear cut line between gathering information and explaining. Let me try to summarize the view which I have been describing and commenting on. The position is that the historians' fundamental concern is explaining how something happened or explaining what happened or telling what happened or describing what happened. These are all closely related if not identical activities. Moreover, they are essentially different than explaining why something happened. These activities are much more like reporting on information gathered then like explaining why something occurred. I have taken the position:

(1) that this could be true without establishing that historians do not explain why things happen.

[3] *Ibid.*

(2) that the process of information gathering is not totally separable from the explanation why process.

(3) that scientists likewise gather information.

Therefore, this does not show that the historian occupies some unusual position.

The most interesting part of the position being considered deserves summarization and commentary. This is the contention that history is non-scientific because we *must* have a non-scientific way of describing how things are in order that explanatory disciplines can get under way. History is slightly sophisticated common sense. Indeed, it does not describe everything or even most things. It is selective. But the important point is that with regard to those events which *are* the object of its concern it does not account for them but merely points them out in such a way that science might account for them.

This thesis is closely related, of course, to the essential dictum of certain types concerned with problems in the philosophy of mind.[4] There the view is that no amount of empirical research can eliminate the use of ordinary mentalistic language because without the non-scientific ways of specifying that which is going on there can be no coherent account of mental phenomena. Suppose we distinguish between showing that ghosts don't really exist on the basis of empirical research and showing what is involved in perceiving a table by virtue of empirical research. In the case of ghosts you are not showing that ghost talk is meaningless but that ghosts don't exist. In the case of tables you are neither showing that table talk is meaningless nor that tables don't exist. Indeed, a presupposition of accounting for that occurrence denoted by the expression "is perceiving a table" is the acceptance of the existence of tables. However, the distinction between showing that there are no ghosts and showing what goes on when you are seeing a table is not so sharp as it might first appear. It seems to me that those who feel the distinction is quite clear are implicitly or explicitly endorsing a sharp distinction between the analytic and

4   For an interesting recent discussion from which I derived a great deal see Richard Rorty, "Mind-Body Identity, Privacy, and Categories", *The Review of Metaphysics*, Vol. XIX, No. 1, pp. 24-54.

the synthetic. As is already apparent from what I have said I cannot endorse this distinction. This is surely not the place to rehearse Quine's arguments against that distinction but it is worth mentioning quite explicitly that I accept what is perhaps an even stronger form of pragmatism than the one tacitly dictated by Quine's arguments.[5] Let me come back to my claim that those who feel there is a sharp distinction between the ghost case and the table case are implicitly or explicitly endorsing the analytic-synthetic distinction. What they seem to assume is that empirical findings cannot affect the meanings of terms in the language. Ordinary language is somehow necessarily sacrosanct. Science presupposes it and here "it" denotes some fairly fixed set of locutions. But it seems to me that this misrepresents things. Science can show that ghosts don't exist but it can also show that ghost talk is meaningless in the sense that ghost talk is part of a general manner of speaking which is far less efficacious than some other ways of talking which disallows ghost talk. In fact, it might well be that science shows that ghosts fail to exist by virtue of this kind of procedure. It is not that in showing that ghosts don't exist we do not bring in empirical data which diminishes the likelihood that they do. Rather, in some ultimate sense, the acceptability of the counter evidence to the ghost hypothesis is an implicit endorsement of that framework which gets on quite well without them. If this happens we can say that in a sense we both have and haven't gotten rid of ghost talk. If getting rid of ghost talk requires getting totally bewildered responses from native speakers when presented with such verbal stimulations as "There's a ghost in my room!" then, indeed, we have not as yet gotten rid of ghost talk. However, this seems to me too strong a condition and, moreover, it might well be that someday soon we shall have gotten rid of ghost talk even in this sense. I hold that we could get rid of table talk in the same way. Perhaps it is less likely. Who is to say? But it seems to me a possibility. What is more important,

5 Willard Van Orman Quine, "Two Dogmas of Empiricism", in *From A Logical Point Of View* (New York and Evanston, Harper and Row, 1963), pp. 20-46. See also the fulfillment of the promise at the end of "Two Dogmas", in *Word and Object* (New York, Technology Press of the Massachusetts Institute of Technology and John Wiley and Sons, 1960).

however, is that getting rid of table talk might come about by virtue of empirical investigation. Incidentally, I see no reason to suppose that we cannot likewise get rid of mental talk. Of course, in the case of ghosts, tables, and desires, something will take its place. But if this happens, then it follows logically that we have gotten rid of it. At this juncture it would be interesting to consider ever so briefly Collingwood and his infamous doctrine of emphatic understanding.[6] Collingwood could be taken as holding to the view that the object of historical study dictates that the methodology of history be unique. He could be taken as committed to the view that explaining the actions of human agents necessitates mental talk and by virtue of this fact one cannot explain in history as one does in true scientific disciplines like physics. As is well known, he speaks of the *inside* and the *outside* of an event and then suggests that the historian must seek to *get at* the inside of the event he is explaining. Only when he succeeds may he justifiably claim to have explained the event in question. Consider the following three theses which present in what is surely an overly succinct manner the basic position of Collingwood.

(1) The historian *need* not and *cannot* (without ceasing to be an historian) emulate the scientist in searching for the causes of events or the laws governing events.

(2) This does not mean that words such as "cause" are necessarily out of place in reference to history; it only means that they are used there in a special sense.

(3) And this (the thought in the mind of the person by whose agency the event came about) is not something other than the event, it is the inside of the event itself.

That the historian *need* not emulate the natural scientist in searching for general laws is, of course, compatible with what has been said so far. He need not because the laws required for his explanations might be those being searched for by natural or social scientists. That the historian *cannot* is to claim that there is

6 R. G. Collingwood, "History as Re-enactment of Past Experience", in *Theories of History*, Patrick Gardiner, editor (Glencoe, Ill., The Free Press, 1959), pp. 249-264.

a decision procedure for deciding between F.O.S.$_1$ and F.O.S.$_2$, viz. always follow F.O.S.$_2$. I see no reason to accept this view. Given some of the findings of modern psychology, there appear to be some reasons for rejecting it. I do not find in Collingwood any strong arguments to support it.

Words like "cause" are not out of place in history. They merely operate in a special sense. What is this special sense? Collingwood might be taken as saying that you are not likely to find, and need not necessarily find, causal laws for historical explanations which are generalizations of conditionals formed by taking descriptions of the antecedent conditions as the antecedent and the description of the event as the consequent. I think this interpretation of Collingwood is substantiated by (3). It is not that there are certain kinds of events which are not really events at all, but rather that certain events have both insides *and* outsides as opposed to just outsides. The metaphorical language used here makes it difficult to feel certain of any interpretation. And this is true of a great deal of Collingwood's work. But the inside-outside dichotomy is best taken, I believe, as referring to two aspects of one and the same event. And this immediately leads me to consider the dichotomy as referring to two different descriptions of one and the same event. If this is correct, I think Collingwood's claim can be taken to be in rough agreement with much of what we have said so far.

The doctrine of *empathetic understanding* has both a methodological and a logical role. As a methodological doctrine it can be helpful for the historian as well as for the psychologist, anthropologist, etc. However, Hempel's advice concerning this method should be taken seriously. It can be carried too far as, perhaps, a reincarnated Aristotelian physicist who suddenly returned to earth might agree. But there is a distinction between emphatizing with falling rain and emphatizing with falling Caesar. There is, however, a logical doctrine associated with *empathetic understanding* which is, on *my* account, a rough prefiguring of some of the modifications to the *covering-law* model suggested throughout. Collingwood is, on this view, a founding father of the *covering-law* school.

The matter of whether you can really state how things happened has been of much concern to historians. The problem of objectivity in history has surely received more attention by historians than has the problem of historical explanation. The two are, as I have been suggesting, closely related issues. And sometimes the historian has failed to notice this. But the problem of historical objectivity, qua that problem, deserves a brief comment or two in the present context simply *because* of its relationship to the problem of historical explanation. One might put the question this way: Is it possible for the historian to give an account of the past which is *true to what really happened*? Obviously, Trevor-Roper, for one, thinks it possible to come closer to this ideal than some historians do.[7] Also he believes that some historians do not come very close at all, e.g. Toynbee and A. J. P. Taylor.[8] Walsh alludes to what might be termed the philosophical problem of historical objectivity. He remarks that "... we are forced to look at the past through the eyes of the present and accommodate what we see to the conceptual scheme we use now...".[9] Notice that Walsh speaks of the past and the present. He could, I believe, just as easily have spoken of the present in two different societies.

Suppose historian S is offering an account of the assassination of the Japanese Prime Minister Hara. The assassination took place in 1921 and so may reasonably be called contemporary history. S is from a western country. He obtains access to the personal belongings of several members of the private staff of the deceased Prime Minister. Included in these belongings are several diaries. S reads these carefully and comes upon one which obviously belonged to a servant in the Hara household. Contained in the servant's diary is a detailed description of many meals involving Hara and distinguished guests including a meal involving Hara

[7] For an interesting, well written account of recent historical controversy as well as an indication of the location of numerous scholarly articles on these matters see Ved Mehta, "The Flight of Crook-Taloned Birds", *New Yorker Magazine*, Dec. 8 and 15, 1962.
[8] *Ibid.*
[9] A worthwhile introductory book is W. H. Walsh, *Philosophy of History: An Introduction* (New York, Harper Torch Book, 1960). See also W. Dray, *Philosophy of History* (New York, Prentice Hall, 1965).

and his assassin which took place on the evening before the assassination. The diary presents a detailed account of the behavior of all those who attended the meal. In reading about the behavior of Hara's assassin S notes that the man servant has commented about the extraordinary amount of eating noise made by the gentleman at the dinner the evening before the assassination. In addition, S has a look at some of Hara's own personal writings in which he more than once comments about the crudeness of western table manners. S, who has always been less than satisfied with the standard accounts of the assassination, starts molding an account of the *true story* based on the evidence he has been examing, *viz.* Hara's fetish about table manners and the assassins *bad table manners*. But S is no Holmes. In fact, he is almost a Watson.[10] S, the westerner, has *deduced* that eating noise at the table is an example of bad table manners. But the Japanese do not consider this to be so. And, since Hara was Japanese, S's undeveloped theory is ill-founded. Perhaps it is true that a Japanese historian would never have been led to begin what S began. But had S been a competent historian he should have likewise refrained from making the illegitimate inference upon which his new theory was to rest. If the problem of historical objectivity simply involved the difficulties of getting all the relevant cultural information in order to write a competent history then the problem is not really a philosophical problem. Moreover, it is surely not unique to history. However, Walsh's talk of conceptual frameworks leads us to believe that he has something more profound in mind. Conceptual framework talk has been commonplace in a great deal of contemporary philosophical literature. However, the discussions of frameworks by such people as Quine do not show that history occupies some unique position amongst the sciences. Walsh would surely agree that man in not simply a passive recipient. He is, indeed, a formulator. What there is, 'tis said, is, in part, a function of our way of looking at things. But on the other hand, our way of looking at things is determined, in part, by how they are. This interplay or spirality gets mirrored in language. And the ties be-

---

[10]   I have in mind here the *motion picture* Watson more than the *literary* Watson.

tween language and reality are such that each must reflect the essential characteristics of the other.

There can be no doubt that all our knowledge begins with experience. For how should our faculty of knowledge be awakened into action did not objects affecting our senses partly of themselves produce representations, partly arouse the activity of our understanding to compare these representations, and, by combining or separating them, work up the raw material of the sensible impressions into that knowledge of objects which is entitled experience? In the order of time, therefore, we have no knowledge antecedent to experience, and with experience all our knowledge begins.
   But though all our knowledge begins with experience, it does not follow that it arises out of experience. For it may well be that even our empirical knowledge is made up of what we receive through impressions and of what our own faculty of knowledge (sensible impressions serving merely as the occasion) supplies from itself.[11]

Kant, in this way, set the stage for a careful critical analysis of knowledge. He begins by accepting the *truism* – so stressed by Hume – that "knowledge begins with experience". However, knowledge is judgmental. And the Humean view, which focuses so hard on the above truism, fails as a successful explication of knowledge in failing to recognize the active role of the *mind* in the knowledge process. The mind, far from being like a movie screen or wax tablet, is a formulator. And even empirical knowledge – knowledge of what there is and what there is is like – is, in part, determined by the active mind. But if "someone knows the book is red" entails " 'the book is red' is true" and if " 'the book is red' is true" is true if and only if the book *is* red, then Kant's characterization of the mind as active becomes more than just an epistemological claim – it becomes an ontological claim. What there is, is, in part, a function of the mind's way of parsing the universe. Talk of the mind and its active role has been replaced in much contemporary literature by conceptual framework talk and the role of language and how it limits what there is. But the fundamental insight is Kantian. It has been clarified, improved

[11] Immanuel Kant, *Critique of Pure Reason*, tr. Norman Kemp Smith (London, Macmillan, 1958), pp. 41-42.

and reacted to. But it is *this insight* which has been reacted to. Much of contemporary philosophy is not so much an attempt to deal with Hume's skepticism as it is an attempt to clarify and analyse Kant's rejoinder to Humean skepticism.

Consider the following summing up from Quine – a contemporary analyst of the very first order:

As an empiricist I continue to think of the conceptual scheme of science as a tool, ultimately, for predicting future experience in the light of past experience. Physical objects are conceptually imported into the situation as convenient intermediaries – not by definition in terms of experience, but simple as irreducible posits comparable, epistemologically, to the gods of Homer. For my part I do, *qua* lay physicist, believe in physical objects and not in Homer's gods; and I consider it a scientific error to believe otherwise. But in point of epistemological footing the physical objects and the gods differ only in degree and not in kind. Both sorts of entities enter our conception only as cultural posits. The myth of physical objects is epistemologically superior to most in that it has proved more efficacious than other myths as a device for working a manageable structure into the flux of experience.[12]

Man makes myth. And the whole of reality is orderable in different ways – in fact, in an infinite number of ways. The picture of man as a passive receiver of impressions from without is hopelessly inaccurate. Man is discriminating. And this is no contingent fact. It is a necessary truth about man. He cannot, in one sense, escape the limits of his myth. But his inability to do so is not a physical limitation on his capacity. (Daily visits to the gym will not improve his chances of pushing outside the framework.)

Yet, paradoxically, though man is aware of the mythic element in the nature of things he is compelled to take the myth seriously. Says Quine in a much later work:

Have we now so far lowered our sights as to settle for a relativistic doctrine of truth – rating the statements of each theory as true for that theory, and brooking no higher criticism? Not so. The saving consideration is that we continue to take seriously our own particular aggregate science, our own particular world-theory or loose total fabric of quasi-theories, whatever it may be.[13]

[12] Quine, *op. cit.*, "Two Dogmas", p. 44.
[13] Quine, *op. cit.*, *Word and Object*, p. 24.

Perhaps a simple example will serve to illustrate the way in which language or the conceptual framework affects what there is. We look around us and observe what there is and how what there is is. Books sit on tables, lamps stand on floors, etc. But what of the book-table which stands on the floor?[14] Are there any book-tables in the room? What, indeed, is a book-table? Why it is simply the object *describable by us* as the combination of the table and the book. But why not a world of book-tables in which books and tables are identified as parts of book-tables? Is there an a priori argument for our way of classifying the segments of the manifold? We enter a primitive society whose language is radically different from our own. Upon meeting a friendly native we begin to translate his language by pointing to objects and attempting to elicit verbal responses. A rabbit goes by. We point to it and the native says "Gavagai". Continued repetition of this performance leads us to make a certain entry in our translation manual – " 'gavagai' means 'rabbit' ". But there *are* no rabbits in our native's world. "Gavagai" is uttered whenever the native observes a part of the universal rabbit. And all rabbits are part of the universal rabbit. But aren't there really rabbits in his world? Are there book-tables in ours? When we come to such basic concepts as *physical object*, *causal relation*, etc. things rapidly become even more complicated.[15]

These observations, as Quine has noted, are not designed to lead us to some sort of conceptual solipsism. Our framework is not totally arbitrary. For one thing the *given*, whatever that is, affects it. But, again, what there is is, *in part*, a function of the framework.

Ontological relativism has many forms, i.e. it has been pointed out and presented in many different ways. But it is possible to distinguish two types of ontological relativism – one of which is a

[14] This example seems to me but a simpler and less interesting case of Goodman's *grue-bleen* and related examples. Moreover, I hope that I am making a closely related, if not the same, point with it. Though he needs no endorsement from me I should like to remark that Goodman's observations centering around the *grue-bleen* discussion seems to me some of the most interesting and important in recent philosophical literature. Davidson and Jeffrey have done a great deal by way of making me appreciate the importance of them.

[15] The rabbit example comes from Quine's *Word and Object*, p. 29.

relativistic ontological relativism. Granting the active role of the mind in imposing certain categories or concepts on the given we may ask whether the categories or concepts imposed are necessary. And if all aren't, are any? Making sure that we are not carried away by the physicalistic metaphor we may ask, "Must all minds impose the same order for all times" or "Must conceptual frameworks be permanent, fixed, immutable?" Our book-table example was designed to show that certain low level concepts, e.g. the concept of *book*, are not necessary to the framework. But are there *any* categories which must be present in and imposed by the mind? Candidates would by such categories or concepts as *causality, physical object, space, time, person.* If there are certain parts of the framework which are necessary then with respect to these it would, perhaps, make no sense to ask "ought we accept them – though they are mythical?" We should be sensitive to the qualitative difference between the following two questions:

(1) Ought we have a concept of book and a concept of table or ought we have a concept of book-table?

and

(2) Ought we have a concept of causality?

What is the alternative in (2)? It is not clear that there is one. And if there isn't then the ought question is a mistake in virtue of the oft-quoted evaluative motto "ought implies can". How do we account for the similarity in our frameworks if the basic categories are not fixed and immutable? C. I. Lewis remarks that,

The coincidence of our fundamental criteria and principles is the combined result of the similarity of human animals, and of their primal interests, and the similarities of the experience with which they have to deal.[16]

Our experiences mold our minds. The framework is ground by experience. But experience is likewise determined by the framework. Another paradox to compound the already paradoxical situation of ontological relativism. Relativistic ontological rela-

[16] C. I. Lewis, *Mind and the World Order* (New York, Dover Publications, 1929), p. 20.

tivism is twice-over paradoxical. Take seriously the mythic and realize that experience forms the mind while being formed *by* the mind!

Our categories are guides to action. Those attitudes which survive the test of practice will reflect not only the nature of the active creature by the general character of the experience he confronts. Thus, indirectly, even what is a priori may not be an exclusive product of "reason", or made in Plato's heaven in utter independence of the world we live in. Moreover, the fact that man survives and prospers by his social habits serves to accentuate and perfect agreement in our basic attitudes. Our common understanding and our common world may be, in part, created in response to our need to act together and to comprehend one another. Critical discussion is but a prolongation of that effort which we make to extend the bounds of successful human cooperation. It is no more necessary to suppose that agreement in fundamental principles is completely ready-made that it is to suppose that infants must already have precisely those ideas which later they find words to express. Indeed our categories are almost as much a social product as is language, and in something like the same sense. It is only the *possibility* of agreement which must be antecedently presumed. The "human mind" is a coincidence of individual minds which partly, no doubt, must be native, but partly is itself created by the social process. Even that likeness which is native would seem to consist in capacities and tendencies to action, not in mental content or explicit modes of thought. That the categories are fundamental in such wise that the social process can neither create nor alter them, is a rationalistic prejudice without foundation. There is much which is profound and true in traditional conceptions of the a priori. But equally it should be clear that there is much in such conceptions which smacks of magic and superstitious nonsense. Particularly it is implausible that what is a priori can be rooted in a "rational nature of man" which is something miraculous and beyond the bounds of psychological analysis and genetic explanation.[17]

On this account the underlying principle of category formation is pragmatic. The categories can be altered. And the alteration of a category or categories hinges on how successful the current ones are serving as guides to actions of all sorts. If they are not serving well they will be changed. The categories are not fixed and immutable. Walsh is, therefore, quite right when he remarks that we must accommodate what we see to out present conceptual scheme.

[17]   *Ibid.*, pp. 21-22.

But this is true in every domain. Moreover, it must not be thought that we are accommodating to our framework *as opposed to* attaining some ideal which would involve a sort of direct confrontation with reality. The changing world, the changing scientific framework, the changing language, all exert forces on one another which makes any explanatory discipline relativistic in a sense. The invention of the thermometer might be said to have changed the meaning of the word "temperature". However, it does not follow that we cannot understand what was meant by *temperature* talk in a pre-thermometal world. Getting down the true view is a complex task. It is not only complex in that there is frequently a great deal to find out but it is methodologically complex in that various types of alterations can be made to make the whole picture most accurate. The historian, like any other scientist, must be cognizant of the fact that he is more than a reporter. It might be thought that Toynbee, for example, is far too conscious of the alternatives to *straight description*. In fact, with reference to D(2), it might be claimed that Toynbee is too frequently presenting how-possiblies rather than how-actualies. I believe this is true. However, the how-possibly, though not an explanation in itself, is surely a possible part of the explanatory process. The presentation of a how-possibly, as I see it, is very much like putting forth a hypothesis which, in history, frequently amounts to suggesting a non-standard description of the complex event. If the historian goes no further he is not fulfilling his obligation as a scientist. For as Toynbee himself has said when considering the claim that he views himself a prophet,

The imputation is difficult to deal with, because the next most ridiculous thing to saying "I think I am a prophet" would be to say "I really don't think I am".[18]

The historian must try to get it right. Giving how-possiblies might serve as a beginning. But there is more to do. Toynbee does more. Whether he succeeds in turning his how-possiblies into bonafide how-actualies I am not prepared to say. I leave that to Mr. Trevor-Roper and other qualified historians. However, he is surely jus-

[18] Arnold Toynbee, *A Study of History*, Vol. 12 (Oxford, Oxford University Press, 1961), p. 5.

tified in offering how-possiblies as part of the explanatory process. If Trevor-Roper objects on the grounds that this is an illegitimate scientific activity I must object. Its legitimacy seems to me unquestionable. Its satisfactoriness – (in Toynbee's case) – seems subject to debate.

I welcome back the how-possibly. It is not a special sort of explanation. Moreover, it is not unique to history. It is a part of the explanatory process.

The intuitionistic suspicion that history is significantly different than other disciplines because of its subject matter seems to me ill-founded. It rests, in part, on a misunderstanding of how other disciplines operate and, more basically, on a misunderstanding as to the nature of things.[19]

Finally we come to examine D(1). Hempel speaks of

... a general *condition of adequacy for any rationally acceptable explanation of a particular event*. That condition is the following: Any rationally acceptable answer to the question 'Why did event X occur?' must offer information which shows that X was to be expected – if not definitely, as in the case of D-N explanation, then at least with reasonable probability. Thus, the explanatory information must provide good grounds for believing that X did in fact occur; otherwise, that information would give us no adequate reason for saying: "That explains it – that does show why X occurred."[20]

Shortly thereafter Hempel adds

It will hardly be necessary to emphasize that it is not, of course, the *purpose* of an explanation to provide grounds in support of the explanandum-statement; for, as was noted in the first section of this essay, a request for an explanation normally *presupposes* that the explanandum-statement is true. The point of the preceding remarks is rather that an adequate explanation cannot help providing information which, if properly established, also provides grounds in support of the explanandum-statement.[21]

We see Hempel, in these remarks, affirming (a) of D(1). Hempel

[19] The crucial point here is that the changing of ontological units *could* alter science and conversely. We are inclined, quite naturally, to be somewhat provincial with regard to our ontological commitments. Thus the *book-table* example as well as the *grue-bleen* example seem easily *reducible*. However, this merely indicates our provincialism.

[20] Hempel, *op. cit.*, "Aspects", p. 368.

[21] *Ibid.*

calls this a *criterion of adequacy* rather than a part of the explication of the concept of explanation. Plainly Hempel would agree that this condition is more pervasive than deductiveness. He concedes that many explanations are statistical *as opposed to* deductive-nomological. However, the condition is apparently labelled a *condition* of adequacy because it is "... necessary but not sufficient for an acceptable explanation."[22] I should agree that this is the case. My reasons, however, are quite different than Hempel's. Moreover, I feel that D(1)a and D(1)b, taken together, are necessary and sufficient conditions. Whether we should call D(1)a and D(1)b a statement of a condition of adequacy or something else I would not care to say. However, it is this *condition* which I take to be the essential feature of explanation.

Hempel believes that experimental data, for example, may support an assumption A without explaining A. He says

Similarly, a set of experimental data may strongly *support* the assumption that the electric resistance of metal increases with their temperature or that a certain chemical inhibits the growth of cancer cells, without providing any *explanation* for these presumptive empirical regularities.[23]

The difficulty, Hempel feels, is that no laws or theoretical principles have been invoked. But it seems to me that in cases like the above you are explaining how something happened or, perhaps, what happened or, more precisely, what is happening. And though explaining-how and explaining-what are not exactly like explaining-why they are alike insofar as they all involve general connecting principles. Suppose, taking Hempel's example, a certain chemical c inhibits the growth of cancer cells. Hempel says that the evidence statements $e_1 \ldots e_n$ might increase our belief that c inhibits the growth of cancer cells but needn't explain why the growth is inhibited. But surely general principles are being tacitly invoked in order for us to recognize that $e_1 \ldots e_n$ is evidence for the claim. These general connecting principles might be vague analogues derived from other experiments of a related sort. But if there are no principles then what grounds can we offer for

22 *Ibid.*
23 *Ibid.*

describing e_k as a piece of evidence which supports the claim that the chemical c inhibits the growth of cancer cells? This, of course, is more than reminiscent of Goodman's notion of parent predicates, et. al., in his discussion of projectability.[24] One can accept this much of Goodman's claim without endorsing the whole of Goodman's position. And given that you grant that there are these *analogue-principles* you should agree that what you have is properly construed as an explanation of what is happening. This seems quite clear in history where, in many cases, the explanation being given is best called an explanation-what. Here again the evidence evinced in favor of the claim that some historical event took place is an explanation of that event and does invoke some general principles which provide the grounds upon which we base the statement that this is indeed evidence in support of the claim that the event in question took place. Therefore, I wish to take (D1)a and D(1)b as conditions of adequacy which are both necessary and sufficient for, at least, *historical* explanation. Moreover, I see no reason not to extend this to include all explanation. Doing so will allow us to resurrect Hempel's thesis of structural identity between explanation and prediction – a thesis which he seems ready to abandon in part. The inclusion of D(1)b was motivated by the desire to eliminate how-possiblies as explanations. However, there are more compelling reasons than this. The most compelling reason that I can think of is that it appears to be accurate. In a real sense, all explanations are explanation sketches. This does not mean that the entailment relationship never holds between *explanans* and *explanandum*. Rather, it means that all explanations can be filled in further – in the various ways mentioned earlier – and are, therefore, such that more information could further increase our degree of belief that the event being explained took place. Remember that the difficulty with the how-possibly wasn't that we could not bring forth more evidence to increase our degree of belief that there was a platform up against the fence or that the centerfielder wore anti-gravity shoes. Surely we could. The problem, however, was that this additional evidence

[24] Nelson Goodman, *Fact, Fiction, and Forecast* (Cambridge, Mass., Harvard University Press, 1955).

could not add credibility to the claim that the catch was possible. If all the statements in an *explanans* are taken as analytic and the *explanandum* follows logically from the *explanans* then I should hold that we have no explanation. I should think Hempel would agree with this. The underlying reason for this is not that the *explanans* must contain empirical statements. This ploy is merely a way of *assuring* that the underlying principle will hold. The principle being upheld is that brought out in D(1). How-possiblies are *like* those *seeming* explanations alluded to above in which all statements in the *explanans* are taken to be analytic and the *explanandum* is entailed by the *explanans*. They are not alike in the sense that we take the *explanans* statement to be analytic but rather in the sense that new evidence cannot increase our belief in the *explanandum-statement* – given that it is possibility statement.

The position may be summarized as follows:

(1) X explains Y if and only if X justifiably increases our degree of belief that Y occurred and X is such that new information could be added to it which would further justifiably increase our belief that Y occurred.

(2) EX_1 is a better explanation of E_k than EX_2 if and only if the explanans of EX_1 justifiably increases our degree of belief that E_k occurred more than does the explanans of EX_2.

On this view there can be many different explanations of the same event. It does not follow that if two explanations, EX_1 and EX_2, of the same event E_k are equivalent they are equally good. Indeed, the task of determining whether two explanations are equivalent is a difficult one. Moreover, the matter of equivalence of increase of belief might enter into the *ultimate* criterion of equivalence of explanation.[25]

---

[25] All this is, of course, intimately related to the notions of *probabilistic inference* and *utility*. I hope eventually to say much more about these matters using R. C. Jeffrey's *The Logic of Decision* (New York, McGraw Hill, 1965), as a starting point.

V

HISTORIANS, FREEDOM AND THE LOGIC
OF PREDICTION

Historians, like other social scientists, display a frequently un-sophisticated interest in the so-called free-will problem. They quite correctly believe that it is relevant to their enterprise. However, many do not have any clear understanding of either what the problem is or how it is related to their field. It is not surprising that social scientists are unclear on the issues here. Philosophers who have been fussing over the question for some time are also unclear. In no area is the "what-precisely-is-the-problem" ploy more apparent than in ethics and within ethics on no issue more than the free-will issue. The above considerations together with the fact that Hempel's thesis of structural identity between ex-planation and prediction has made it good form to discuss pre-diction whenever you discuss explanation leads me to include this section.

Some so-called determinists feel committed to no more or, if you prefer, *no less* than the thesis that all behavior is, in principle, explainable and predictable. Somehow the claim about explain-ability seems less obnoxious to laymen and some social scientists than does the claim about predictability. That is, there are some who feel that whereas the fact that an event can be explained in some detail after it has taken place does not *interfere* with man's freedom, the fact that it can be accurately predicted before it took place does. The arguments which purport to show that free-will is compatible with both explainability and predicability in principle are common place in contemporary philosophical lite-rature. The origins of the compatibility thesis go back some time – probably to Hobbes. I have no intention of reviewing these arguments.[1] However, it is this thesis that I endorse though I should by no means agree with all the arguments put forth in its favor. What I would like to do is present some remarks which indicate my position and consider its relationship to the logic of historical inquiry and the logic of prediction.

That the historian must be concerned with the logic of prediction seems apparent. For though the historian does not frequently make *predictions* he is constantly making *retrodictions*, i.e. 'predicting' at some time t_n what 'will' happen at time t_n-1 on the basis of information available only at time t_n-2. And the logic of this *activity* would seem to have an obvious relationship to the logic of genuine prediction. Moreover, if explanation and prediction are *structurally identical* and the historian is concerned with explanation he seems automatically committed to being concerned with prediction.

The remarks that follow were motivated by considering certain *prima facie* similarities between *predicting* and *promising*.[2] In trying to show that uttering a statement of the form "I predict that y" is not a sufficient condition for making a prediction one notices a certain feature of prediction, namely, its conditional character. This observation leads to the presentation of two possible analyses of prediction – the conditional and the conjunctive. The conditional analysis tends to support a certain formulation of the free-will doctrine. The conjunctive analysis tends to support a certain form of determinism.

What began, in my own mind, as little more than a "fussy

---

[1] For some discussions of these matters see *Freedom and the Will*, edited by D. F. Pears (London, Macmillan and Co., 1965).

[2] A great deal of what follows on the next few pages was originally presented as a paper called "Two Analyses of Prediction", at the meetings of the Western Division of the American Philosophical Association at Milwaukee, Wisconsin, May 2, 1964. The paper, under the same name, is also to appear in a forthcoming issue of *Theoria*. Some parts of my discussion were obviously influenced by a paper read at the 1963 meetings of the Western Division of the American Philosophical Association by Michael Scriven. The earlier parts of my paper concerning *predicting* and *promising* had already been written when I heard Scriven's paper. Some of his ideas led me to re-examine what I had been dealing with. I am very much indebted to him.

little *semantical* exercise" leads to a possible "solution" to the free will-determinism issue.

One might hold the following:

(1) A sufficient condition for making a prediction is saying "I predict that y" – where y is a future tensed sentence.

As with promising, where saying "I promise to A" is to promise, so, saying "I predict that y" is to predict. It is not necessarily to predict correctly. But it is to predict.

We wish to examine this claim, i.e. to answer the following question: In which case(s), if any, is the utterance of the words "I predict" followed by a declarative future-tense sentence not a prediction?

Consider the following example:

A and B are arguing whether or not all human behavior is predictable. B says it is. A says it is not. Suddenly, A rises from the chair and says that he has left his cigarettes in the car and is off to get them. As he walks out the door he says to B, "You can't tell whether or not I'll be back." A smiles, his point proven conclusively.

Clearly, it might be argued, the sentence formed by substituting "predict" for "tell" in A's remark, namely, "You can't predict whether or not I'll be back" is false. B need merely have replied to A as he left the house, "I predict you'll be back" in order to prove A wrong. Although A might never have returned to the house, which would have made B's prediction wrong, it would nevertheless be the case that B had made a prediction about A's behavior. Predictions may be wrong. But their being wrong does not impugn the fact that they are predictions.

Let us return to A and B. A is at the door about to leave. He has remarked, "You can't tell whether or not I'll be back." B responds before A gets the door closed, "I predict you'll be back." A scratches his head and says, "I mean *correctly* predict." B's wife, overhearing the conversation, jumps in quickly with "I predict you won't be back." Now A is really perplexed. He resolves his perplexity by staying on and arguing that both B and his wife were wrong, since in order for it to be true either that he will or won't come back, he must first of all have gone. Mr. B. has said,

"I predict you'll be back." If A stays is B's seeming prediction a prediction? If it is not then we have a counter-example to (1).

We might say that A's staying on after B and his wife had made their remarks makes their predictions wrong, rather than making their seeming predictions no predictions at all. This position has a certain appeal. In B's case, for example, it relieves us of saying that what was a prediction stopped being one – or never was one – because of A's remark. It should be noted that the AB affair is a *variant* case. The *normal* case is where the appropriate circumstances are events, conditions, attitudes, beliefs, etc., that exist *prior to or at the same time as* the utterance. A added something after the utterance had been made. He stayed on. A normal case is typified by the following:

(2) Someone predicts that the King of France will have soup for breakfast tomorrow.

Consider the case of the man who seemingly predicts (at time t_1, where t_1 equals April 5, 1740) that the King of France will have soup for breakfast tomorrow. (One *seemingly predicts* when one utters the words "I predict" followed by a future tensed sentence. It should be clear that not all predictions are seeming predictions. We can predict without using the expression "I predict". The question is, are all *seeming predictions* predictions?) Compare this case to the case of a man who seemingly makes the same prediction at time t_2, where time t_2 equals April 5, 1940. Suppose the King did not have soup on the morning of April 6, 1740. Now at the time of the first utterance, t_1, it was possible for the prediction to be correct – though it happened to turn out to be false. But the prediction at t_2 could not possibly have turned out to be right. Thus, one might hold that a sufficient condition for making a prediction is uttering the words, "I predict y" where y describes a *possible future* state of affairs. If y doesn't then this utterance is a seeming but not a real prediction. And, we should have shown that not all utterance of type (1) are predictions. This will not do, however. At any rate, this example won't do it. For, although it is impossible for the King of France to have soup tomorrow unless he is alive tomorrow (and we may even add that it is impossible for the King of France to be alive tomorrow if he is dead today), it is not impossible that the King of France be alive today.

The answer to our original question must wait on further analysis of *prediction*. The problem posed and the brief remarks made about it suggest certain features of the concept of prediction which need mirroring in analysis.[3]

The prediction, "The King of France will have soup for breakfast tomorrow", may be taken as equivalent to either:

A: There will be a King of France alive tomorrow and he will have soup for breakfast.

or

B: If there is a King of France alive tomorrow, he will have soup for breakfast.

Suppose X and Y make a bet on what the King of France will have for breakfast tomorrow. X says that he will have soup for breakfast. If the parties accept A as equivalent to the statement C made in making the bet, namely, "The King of France will have soup for breakfast tomorrow", then, I should think, X would be declared the loser of the bet. However, if they accepted B as the correct interpretation, then, I should think, the bet would be off. Y would not be the winner because, after all, the bet was not that the conditional B is true. Rather, it was a prediction contingent upon the antecedent condition of the King's being alive tomorrow.[4] Certainly A and B are not equivalent translations of "The King of France will have soup for breakfast tomorrow". A involves two predictions; B involves one, at most. Does B involve a prediction at all? Is "I predict B" a prediction?

In order to answer this we should consider the more general claim that

---

[3] Clearly a full analysis of *prediction* or *predicting* would bring in intentions, etc. Does the predictor intend his remark to be a prediction, a disguised conditional, etc.? The actor who says, on stage, "I predict his head will fall" has not predicted. In this respect predicting is like promising. Our discussion will systematically stand clear of these problems.

[4] I had the good fortune to be able to discuss this with Michael Dummett. His views on this matter helped to clarify my position.

(i) I predict x ⊃ y

is equivalent to

(ii) x ⊃ I predict that y.

If we can show (i) equivalent to (ii) then we will have indicated cases where saying "I predict that y" is not necessarily to make a prediction. More accurately, if we take the conditional analysis as correct then saying "I predict that y" under *any* circumstances is not *necessarily* to make a prediction. The difficulty in showing (i) equivalent to (ii) is, of course, intimately related to the more general problem of understanding the conditional. Quine reports the following suggestion of Rhinelander's in a footnote to *Methods of Logic*.

An affirmation of the form "if p then q" is commonly felt less as an affirmation of a conditional than as a conditional affirmation of the consequent. If, after we have made such an affirmation, the antecedent turns out true, then we consider ourselves committed to the consequent, and are ready to acknowledge error if it proves false. If on the other hand the antecedent turns out to have been false, our conditional affirmation is as if it had never been made.[5]

Quine goes on to say that when the antecedent of a conditional is false, the truth value of a conditional becomes more arbitrary than when the antecedent is true. But the "decision which proves most *convenient* (italics mine) is to regard all conditionals with false antecedents as true". I agree with Quine that this decision with regard to conditional *assertions* is the most convenient one. But Rhinelander's interpretation might be most *convenient* for an analysis of conditional *predictions*.

First a brief remark about the syntax of (i). It might be thought that (i) is a rather odd locution. Perhaps, a more acceptable way of putting (i) is

(iii) I predict that, if x, y,

or even

(iv) I predict that y, if x.

Both (iii) and (iv) are, I believe, equivalent to (i) and more clearly

[5]   Willard Van Orman Quine, *Methods of Logic* (New York, Henry Holt and Company, Inc., 1950), p. 12.

bring out the fact that here is a case where the prediction is conditional rather than a case where a conditional is predicted. In both (iii) and (iv) it seems clear that "if x" goes with "I predict that" rather than with "y".

Two questions come to mind. (1) What sorts of things do we predict? (By "sort of thing" I mean what type of entity, e.g., we perceive books, tables, chairs, etc. – the types or sorts of things we perceive are physical objects.) And (2) what conditions make a prediction correct? What we predict are events or states of affairs. We predict that the sun will rise tomorrow, that Glenn will orbit the earth in 89 minutes, that A will return with his cigarettes. Now, although both "x" and "y" may describe events or states of affairs, it is not at all clear what event is described by "x ⊃ y".

But suppose it is claimed that (i) is used to assert that the sentence "x ⊃ y" is true. Taking predicting to be approximately synonymous with the forecasting of a future happening, this account misses out on at least one count. The truth of "x ⊃ y" is, so to speak, timeless, and therefore the interpretation of (i) as predicting that the sentence "x ⊃ y" is true fails to mirror an essential characteristic of prediction, *viz.*, what are predicted are future events, happenings, etc., and predictions are correct, true, etc., if the predicted events occur. Suppose, however, the claim is that the prediction is that the sentence "x ⊃ y" *will be found true*. On this analysis one *is* predicting a future state of affairs. But we must ask whether the prediction, so interpreted, would be correct if "x ⊃ y" is found to be true in virtue of finding "x" false. I have argued that it would not be. Might the above position be modified to accommodate this objection in the following way: "I predict x ⊃ y" means " 'x ⊃ y' will be found true in virtue of finding both "x" and "y" true." But we may still ask whether the prediction is correct if "x" is found false. I hold that it is not. What we must do, I feel, is give up this attempt and recognize that the conditional we have been considering is not the material conditional – it is not fully truth functional. If it were we should have to take the conditional prediction as correct when the antecedent is falsified. Our solution has amounted to introducing a new kind of conditional, à la Rhinelander, which we might call the *truncated conditional.*[6] The truncated conditional is a quasi-material conditional in the sense that it is truth functional only when the antecedent is true. When the antecedent is false the conditional is not to be construed as truth functional.

Consider the case of Mr. C, who tends to forget what day of the week it is, but knows, all too well, that his wife serves chicken for dinner every Saturday night. On a certain afternoon Mr. C predicts that he will have chicken for dinner that evening. When dinner time comes his wife serves him hamburgers. Mr. C is astonished and asks his wife to account for this change of menu for the Saturday night dinner. "But today is Friday", declares Mrs. A.

"Oh!" says Mr. C, "Had I known that, I would never have predicted that we were going to have chicken for dinner this evening." Had Mr. C been more careful that afternoon and said, "I predict that if today is Saturday, we will have chicken for dinner this evening", and had a friend pointed out that it was, in fact, Friday, then Mr. C's response, I claim, would have been in keeping with the remark he made at the dinner table. He would have said, "Consider, then, that I have made no prediction at all."

Should we hold Mr. C to his prediction merely because he did not *present* his prediction in the form of a conditional? On the conditional analysis of prediction, all predictions are conditionals. Mr. C would be *genuinely* wrong if it were Saturday and his wife had decided to vary the menu. The conditional analysis has the virtue of reflecting the distinction between being *trivially* wrong and being genuinely wrong.

Let us return to A and B at the door. If A doesn't leave he might contend that the predictions of both B and his wife are wrong. Here he is interpreting predictions as in A, i.e., conjunctively. On this account B's prediction is correct if A goes and returns. Interpreted in this way B's saying "I predict that y" amounted to his making a prediction. But B might be anxious to interpret his prediction conditionally. If A stays, then B claims he has made no prediction. For his predictive statement should have

[6]   My former colleague, Jerome Schiller, has suggested that this conditional be called the *debased* conditional. (He is also responsible for *truncated* conditional.)

been taken to mean, "If you go for your cigarettes, then you will be back." On this view B's saying "I predict that y" does not amount to making a prediction. On the conjunctive interpretation, predicting is similar to promising. The conditional interpretation holds that the utterance "I predict that y" is an expression of someone's willingness to predict. Whether the person has made a prediction depends on whether or not the antecedent conditions are satisfied. Before we can determine whether saying "I predict that y" commits one to a prediction we must determine the correct analysis of prediction.

If an agent promises to go to the store if his mother gets back before nine, we are correct in saying that he has made a promise even if his mother gets back after nine. He has made a promise all right, but he is not obliged to keep it. Similarly, if the watchmaker guarantees his product but specifies certain conditions that must be satisfied by the consumer, e.g., that he must not step on the watch, the guarantee is made even if the consumer steps on the watch. However, in this case the watch-maker is not obliged to honor the guarantee. The notions of *promising* and *guaranteeing* have the related notions *not obliged to keep* and *not obliged to honor*, respectively, which would lead to a *performatory* analysis of promising and guaranteeing. But predicting has nothing analogous to the concepts *not obliged to keep* and *not obliged to honor*. Predicting is more closely related to betting.

Mr. A goes to the two dollar window, puts down two dollars and says to the teller, "I'm betting that, if it isn't raining at post time, Black Beauty will win." The teller puts the two dollars aside and at post time checks the weather. If it is raining, he returns the two dollars. No bet has been made.

Predicting, like betting, has a performatory aspect. But it is not perfectly analogous to promising because *promisings* are best construed conjunctively and *predictings* conditionally.

In effect we have been considering two possible explications of prediction, *viz.* (a) the conditional and (b) the conjunctive. On (a) all predictions are disguised conditionals. They are conditional in the sense that the prediction *is* a conditional and not *of* a conditional. It is a conditional prediction and not a prediction of a conditional. Thus, asserting "I predict that y" is not a sufficient condition for predicting.

Our remarks about predicting and promising began by considering a hypothetical dispute, *viz.* the dispute concerning the predictability of all human behavior between A and B. What about this dispute? Does the distinction between the conjunctive and the conditional senses of prediction help in determining whether A or B is correct?

A said that not all human behavior was predictable. B claimed it was. B then predicted that A would return and A was forced to change his position by saying that not all human behavior was correctly predictable. Now Mrs. B predicts what she takes to be the contradictory of what B predicted. A decides to stay and thus show both B and his wife wrong. Does A succeed? If he does then the free-will people have gained an *important* victory. Determinism, as we have suggested, is often taken, in part, as the position that all human behavior is, in principle, correctly predictable. Has A shown that this statement of determinism is wrong? If we take prediction conjunctively, then B and his wife have both made predictions. But they are both wrong. This might seem peculiar since Mrs. B's statement appeared to be the contradictory of Mr. B's. But interpreting prediction *either* conjunctively *or* conditionally it was not. B's prediction taken conjunctively was

(1) You will go and you will come back.

Mr. B's prediction was

(2) You will go and you will not come back.[7]

A's action – or lack of it – has mitigated the force of Mrs. B's remark. He falsified the first conjunct of (1) and (2). She has not correctly predicted A's behavior. But if the B's had a son available he could have said "I predict you won't go" and thereby assured one correct prediction of A's behavior. The conjunctive interpretation of prediction favors the determinist thesis.

[7]   See Ayer's discussion of "My friend has stopped writing to me", in Alfred J. Ayer, *Language, Truth and Logic* (New York, Dover Publications, Inc., 1946), p. 76.

On the face of it the conditional analysis favors the libertarian view. On this analysis A *has* prevented two predictions – Mr. and Mrs. B's – of his behavior by altering the circumstances covered by the implicit antecedent of Mr. and Mrs. B's predictions. We remarked earlier that the AB affair was a variant case. It was variant because A *changed* the circumstances after the seeming prediction. And on the conditional interpretation this can void a seeming prediction. The free will-determinist problem, at least in this form, seems to turn on what the correct analysis of prediction is. When A claims that his behavior cannot be predicted he means that he can so alter the conditions that the predictors seeming prediction is not a prediction at all. We said earlier that A might be most anxious to take the conjunctive interpretation and B the conditional. *But they would have been wrong to do so!* A should hold to the conditional analysis of prediction and B should support the conjunctive analysis.

Suppose B – the determinist – made the obvious suggestion that we avoid letting the agent know what our seeming prediction is. This was, after all, the problem in the AB affair. Then, he cannot alter the appropriate circumstances and thereby make our seeming prediction no prediction at all. A can reply by pointing out that since B admits the possibility of keeping the information from the agent he must likewise admit the possibility of the agent getting the information. Thus, says A, all human behavior is not, in principle, predictable. For the persons whose behavior we are seemingly predicting *could* always hear of the seeming prediction and then alter the circumstances.

But, at least one serious problem remains. Suppose the B-child predicts A won't go and we accept the conditional analysis. Indeed, on the conditional view A has voided *two* predictions. But has he a way of preventing the B-child's prediction candidate from being an actual prediction? If not, then even the conditional analysis ultimately favors the weak determinist thesis. Another way of putting this same puzzle is this: How can we translate the B-child's prediction – "He won't go" – into a conditional. On the conditional analysis *all* predictions are disguised conditionals. If the B-child's predictions could be transformed then A could, most likely, alter the antecedent circumstances. You could turn

(1) He won't go

into

(2) If he stays, he won't go.

But if the antecedent of (2) is false, then A goes. So that though the B-child's seeming prediction is no prediction, Mr. and Mrs. B's seeming predictions are. Furthermore, either Mr. or Mrs. B's prediction is correct.

The translation I have to offer of "He won't go" is somewhat precarious. Suppose we take B-child's prediction "He won't go" as

If "he" has a referent, then I predict he won't go.

If A should disintegrate then B-child should not be taken as having incorrectly predicted though A didn't stay. On the other hand, A didn't go, i.e., he didn't leave. The problem, at this level, seems to become entangled in the Russell-Strawson dispute over the proper interpretation of sentences of the form "The so-and-so is such-and-such."[8] The conditional analysis is most compatible with the Strawsonian approach whereas the conjunctive analysis is most compatible with the Russell approach.

I have not supplied a procedure for formulating all predictions in their conditional form. And lacking one we do not know how we should answer the following two questions.

(1) Is there such a procedure?

(2) Will this procedure yield translations which are acceptable?

On the conditional analysis, however, we can at least say that *some* predictions can be vitiated by the agent's actions.

In the preceding remarks I have been talking about the logic of predictions as opposed to the logic of predictive arguments. The structural identity thesis which Hempel espoused was to have held between explanatory and predictive arguments. Scheffler has pointed out a number of significant differences between pre-

---

[8] See Bertrand Russell, "On Denoting", in *Readings in Philosophical Analysis*, Herbert Feigl and Wilfred Sellars, editors (New York, Appleton-Century-Crofts, Inc., 1949), pp. 103-118; P. F. Strawson, "On Referring", in *Essays in Conceptual Analysis*, Anthony Flew, editor (London, Macmillan and Co., Ltd., 1956), pp. 21-52.

diction and explanations.[9] However, Hempel's general attitude is that many of Scheffler's comments simply show that explanations and predictions taken as statements rather than arguments are not structurally identical. However, Hempel, as we have said, considers that his claim has to do with arguments. Letting E(A), P(A), E(S) and P(S) and for "explanatory argument", "predictive argument", "explanatory statement", and "predictive statement" respectively, Hempel's structural identity thesis may be put as follows:

S.I.T.: E(A) at t_l iff P(A) at t_l-n (where n is greater than the interval between t_l and E_k (E_k is the event being explained or predicted).

In one of Scheffler's arguments against equating E(S) and P(S) he considers the *sentence* S.

S: Eisenhower elected President on November 4, 1952. No utterance of S after November 4, 1952 explains Eisenhower's election though every utterance of S prior to November 4, 1952 is a prediction of his victory. This observation of Scheffler's seems quite correct. It is not, of course, a counter example to S.I.T. Utterances of S are neither E(A)'s nor P(A)'s. A P(A) for S would look something like this.

a. Eisenhower is a popular American.
b. Stevenson has too much education.
c. . . .
Therefore, S.

If S.I.T. is true, an E(A) for S would involve a', b', etc. which are like a, b, etc. except for tense. An utterance of S is not an argument at all. The reason why an utterance of S is not an explanation would appear to be that it merely describes what happened, i.e. it is an *explanandum* without an *explanans*. In order to discredit S.I.T. one must show that there is some predictive argument which could not properly serve as an explanatory argument.[10] It has been

[9]   Israel Scheffler, "Explanation, Prediction and Abstraction", *British Journal for the Philosophy of Science*, 7 (1957), pp. 293-309.
[10]   We are considering only *half* of S.I.T., *viz.* the claim that every prediction could serve as an explanation. Many have objected to the other *half*,

pointed out by both Scheffler and Scriven that certain sound predictive arguments of a non-deductive character are not potentially explanatory arguments. From the appropriate statistical data we may properly predict the number of male births, traffic deaths, etc. But these do not afford explanations of what they served to predict. According to Hempel what would bar the predictive argument from being a potential explanatory argument is

... the fact that they do not invoke any general laws either of strictly universal or of statistical form; it appears to be characteristic of an explanation, though not necessarily of a prediction, that it presents the inferred phenomena as occurring in conformity with general laws.[11]

In "Aspects of Scientific Explanation", Hempel, discussing the same question remarks that

... the predictions in our illustrations proceed from an observed sample of a population to another, as yet unobserved one; and on some current theories of probabilistic inference such arguments do not depend upon the assumption of general empirical laws. According to Carnap's theory of inductive logic, for example, such inferences are possible on purely logical grounds; the information about the given sample confers a definite logical probability upon any proposed prediction concerning an as yet unobserved sample. On the other hand, certain statistical theories of probabilistic inference eschew the notion of purely logical probabilities and qualify predictions of the kind here considered as sound only on the further assumption that the selection of individual cases from the total population has the character of a random experiment with certain general statistical characteristics. But that assumption, when explicitly spelled out, has the form of a general law of statistical-probabilistic form; hence, the predictions are affected by means of covering-laws after all.[12]

Hempel concludes this paragraph by saying that

... Thus construed, even the predictions here under discussion turn out to be (incompletely formulated) potential explanations.[13]

I am struck by the fact that this manner of preserving S.I.T. is,

viz. the claim that every explanation is also a potential prediction. Hempel seems to me to have undermined these objections while recognizing their interest. See "Aspects", pp. 364-74.

[11]   Hempel, op. cit., "Deductive", p. 119.
[12]   Hempel, op. cit., "Aspects", p. 376.
[13]   Ibid.

in some sense, incompatible with Hempel's arguments against accepting the condition of adequacy, discussed earlier, as sufficient. The argument there was that sometimes our degree of belief can justifiably be increased without it being the case that we have an explanation and this was the case because no laws or connecting principles were invoked in the examples chosen. But those examples were rather like the examples under consideration here. If laws are tacitly invoked here then why not there? And if there then why the claim that those examples are not explanations? [14] My recommended modification of the covering-law model seems to have the affect of resurrecting the structural identity thesis. Hempel's problem seems to me to arise from his having focused almost exclusively on explanation-why. This leads Hempel to concentrate on *causal* explanation. [15] The predictions under consideration here are structurally identical with explanations-what. But the essential feature with respect to which they are structurally identical is that outlined in D(1). And the characterization of explanation (and prediction) contained in D(1) makes it quite plain that there is no incompatibility between so-called free will and determinism – where determinism is the doctrine that all behavior is, in principle, explainable and predictable.

Obviously we have started across the very short bridge which connects epistemology or philosophy of science and ethics. I feel obliged to bring us at least to the toll gate which stands on the other side. I cannot refrain from grinding a final axe while making the crossing. The narrowmindedness of too many analytic philosophers has *sheltered* them from the insights of those most dense of all possible contemporary intellectuals, the existentialist. [16] Philosophical problems, which I find difficult to locate and still more difficult to resolve, should be subjectable to all possible types of investigation. I share with Goodman the view that no methodological stone should be left unturned if insight can be gained

---

[14] Here again it must be noted that, as Hempel points out, one of the crucial notions that requires examination in far greater detail is that of *probabilistic inference*.

[15] The absence of the word "cause" from this essay is not an oversight.

[16] I thank my former colleague William Spanos for stimulating my interest in Sartre.

by the employment thereof. So much by way of polemic.[17]

The relativism that provokes the existentialistic response is an *ontological* rather than an *ethical* one. Perhaps disagreement between people or peoples over ethical issues – a fact on which ethical relativists focus – interests the existentialist. But the existential attitude does not evolve from any series of perceptual observations of the world. It is not based on empirical facts. It is not contingent. God's death was not *seen*. Precisely for this reason existentialism is a philosophical position. And, only insofar as it focuses on a supposed feature of *the nature of things* does it remain a philosophical view.

Ethical relativism has taken many forms. I shall not undertake to thoroughly examine even one statement of it. Rather I shall sketch the view of a *straw* ethical relativist. Then I shall subject my straw man to a shallow attack by an almost equally straw analyst. It is not that I do not believe there are real relativists who come close to my imaginary one. Nor do I believe that my artificial analyst has no point. On the contrary, he has the correct point – the true view! But I call both relativist and analyst *straw* only because I do not deem it necessary to make them of stronger stuff for my present purposes. However, I must introduce them to be able to compare and contrast ethical relativism with ontological relativism.

It is a fact that members of different societies disagree as to whether one and the same object is good or action right. There is frequently *intra*-societal disagreement. But total disagreement between all the members of a society A and all the members of society B – total *inter*-societal disagreement – as to the rightness of some action *a* is the objective foundation of ethical relativism. From this fact the relativist argues as follows: Total disagreement on the matter of the rightness of *a* between all A's and all B's can be accounted for only by the fact that A's and B's mean something different by *rightness*. The *right* and the *good* are relative to the

---

[17] The remarks that follow are not only relevant because the free will issue is considered. Hopefully they will serve as something of an analogical argument. A great deal of what follows appeared originally in an article called "The Origins of Sartre's Existentialism", in *Ethics*, April, 1966.

community in a way which *six-inchedness* is not. This point both emerges from and explains the possibility, and sometimes actuality, of total disagreement. So states our straw relativist.

Our straw analyst counters. If there is genuine disagreement between all A's and all B's then *right* must mean the same in both societies. If *right* did not mean in A-land what it means in B-land then it would be senseless to speak of a genuine disagreement in values. If Jones and Smith disagree as to whether Edwards has red hair, the disagreement – to be genuine – must presuppose agreement as to the meaning of the terms or concepts used in the statement of the proposition, i.e., "Edwards has red hair". If Jones means by *red* what Smith means by *green*, then their disagreement is not a genuine factual disagreement but one which turns on the meanings of the concepts employed. Likewise the disagreement between the members of A-land and the members of B-land might turn out to be analogous to Jones and Smith disagreeing on the meanings of concepts. But then it would not be a genuine moral conflict. More importantly, it would be impossible for the relativist to suppose the disagreement is of this sort. For if he did, he would be assuming what he is attempting to establish!

Ontological relativism is not contingent. It is – paradoxically – absolutely relativistic. The doctrine of ontological relativism makes its appearance in a great deal of contemporary philosophical thought. It is, in fact, a dominant theme. Sartre's existentialistic position has as its philosophical cornerstone this doctrine. The reactions to the doctrine vary from the cold, passive reaction of a Quine to the anguished emotional reaction of a Sartre. And, perhaps, the existential *attitude* is the *essence* of existentialism. But the view which provokes the attitude is shared by existentialist and analyst.

Let us briefly consider the development of the existentialist position in some of the writings of Jean-Paul Sartre. Existence precedes essence. This is the credo of the existentialist. "... or, if you prefer", says Sartre, "that subjectivity must be the starting point".[18] In explicating the meaning of this view Sartre asks us to

[18]   Jean-Paul Sartre, *Existentialism*, tr. Bernard Frechtman (New York, Philosophical Library, 1947), p. 15.

consider a manufactured object – a book or a paper-cutter. The manufactured object requires a manufacturer. And the manufacturer has, in mind, the essence of the object prior to his bringing it into existence. Its essence, then, precedes its existence. If God were present to serve as manufacturer man could be characterized as just another manufactured object. But for the atheistic existentialist God is dead. Sartre notes how curious it is that the 18th Century philosophers discarded the idea of *God* but retained the doctrine of man's essence preceding his existence. *Even* Kant, says Sartre, did this. Characterizing Kant's position, Sartre says,

Man has a human nature; this human nature, which is the concept of the human, is found in all men, which means that each man is a particular example of a universal concept, man. In Kant, the result of this universality is that the wild man, the natural man, as well as the bourgeois, are circumscribed by the same definition and have the same basic qualities.[19]

But according to Sartre the elimination of God leads to the view that, at least in one being, existence *precedes* essence. There is "... a being who exists before he can be defined by any concept ..."[20] Man turns up on the scene and only afterwards defines himself. Man is the creator of concepts and hence must exist *prior to* the creation of the concept of *man*.

Moreover, man's choices, which are necessarily free, since there are no limitations imposed by a prior conception, create not only one's own image but an image of man in general. Our choices make man. But man can change, for our choices are free. The existentialist believes that man "is condemned every moment to invent man".[21] Furthermore, "... things will be as man will have determined they are to be".[22] And still later, "... there is a universality of man; but it is not given, it is perpetually being made".[23]

Consider next the following remarks by Sartre:

Has anyone ever asked [the painter], "What painting ought he to make?" It is clearly understood that there is no definite painting to

19   *Ibid.*, p. 17.
20   *Ibid.*, p. 18.
21   *Ibid.*, p. 28.
22   *Ibid.*, p. 37.
23   *Ibid.*, pp. 46-7.

be made, that the artist is engaged in the making of his painting, and that the painting to be made is precisely the painting he will have made. It is clearly understood that there are no *a priori* aesthetic values, but that there are values which appear subsequently in the coherence of the painting, in the correspondence between what the artist intended and the result. . . . Painting can be judged only after it has once been made. What connection does that have with ethics? We are in the same creative situation.[24]

The freedom that is man's is not limited. Certain obstacles which seem to limit man's freedom are considered by Sartre when he examines the notion of *facticity*.[25] Sartre argues against these seeming obstacles in an interesting and most *revealing* way. A mountain is an obstacle only if one has chosen to go somewhere which requires crossing it. Says Sartre, "A particular crag, which may manifest a profound resistence if I wish to displace it, will be on the contrary a valuable aid if I want to climb upon it in order to look over the countryside."[26]

Plantinga makes the following observation about the Sartrian position:

Structureless and without form, the in-itself [stuff out there: material stuff] is like Aristotle's prime matter. And therefore, says Sartre, I *choose* my world. For I give to it whatever characteristics it actually has. I constitute it as a world characterized by the law and structure it exhibits. And I do this as a free individual. This is what distinguishes Sartre from any kind of Kantianism: for Sartre, the structure imposed by the for-itself [the stuff inside; mental stuff] upon the in-itself does not flow from any kind of inner necessity, nor are they given in the nature of reason.[27]

But Lewis' view is certainly a "kind of Kantianism". Yet Sartre's view, as I see it, comes very close – in its origin – to Lewis'.

Plantinga offers some arguments to show that Sartre's ethical position is inconsistent with any kind of morality. He says

---

[24] *Ibid.*, p. 50. It must also be noted that science is in the same creative position.

[25] Jean-Paul Sartre, *Being and Nothingness*, tr. Hazel Barnes (New York, Philosophical Library, 1956), p. 482.

[26] *Ibid.*

[27] Alvin Plantinga, "An Existentialist's Ethics", *The Review of Metaphysics*, Vol. XII, No. 2 (Dec. 1958), p. 246.

For Sartre, *every* action, *every* choice, is necessarily right. But morality presupposes that there is something morally at stake when I choose or act; there is the possibility of right and wrong, better or worse. For Sartre these distinctions disappear; the notion of a wrong action is for him analytically impossible.[28]

I am impressed by how close this argument against Sartre comes to the straw analyst's argument against the straw ethical relativist. Plantinga views Sartre's views as essentially ethical. In doing so, I fear he has offered a counter-argument which, though telling, distorts the real point of Sartre's existentialism. Let me attempt to justify my feeling that Plantinga's argument bears a family resemblance to the straw analyst's argument. The analyst argued that genuine disagreement supposed agreement on the meaning of *right*. And Plantinga argues that disagreement between people cannot exist side by side with a view in which what is right means what I choose. If the people of A-land and B-land disagree on whether action *a* is right, there must be agreement between them as to what is meant by *right*. Analogously, if X and Y disagree on whether *a* is right there must be a common definition of *right*. But on Sartre's account there is none. And, furthermore, there can be none.

Let me now sketch what I take to be Sartre's position. Sartre plainly sees man as the imposer of form on the in-itself. Hence, man makes his world in a sense. In fact, he makes his world in precisely the sense in which Kant, Quine, and Lewis believe man makes his world. But Sartre sees in Kant a serious mistake. Kant, according to Sartre, sees man as somehow pre-determined to make it a certain way. But man need not employ any *particular* set of categories. He is free to change the world. Here Sartre stands with Quine and Lewis. He is plainly a *relativistic ontological relativist*. Moreover, I contend he is a relativistic ontological relativist in Lewis' sense. The guiding principle of change is pragmatic. What framework will best do the job? What framework will serve man best? Taking this as the under-lying principle of category change entails man's freedom of choice. The nature of man – along with the nature of everything else – emerges from man's choices. This

[28]   *Ibid.*, p. 248.

is apparent in Sartre's consideration of *facticity*. But the puzzlement is particularly striking when we consider man as the maker of the concept of *man*. The notion on which we must focus is that of *priority*. Sartre's picture of things has man – undefined – existing *temporally* prior to his essence. But he *cannot* and *need not* have this. He cannot have it for man is defined for him by his actions. And his actions define man. Inactive man is not a man. Active man is a man – but then there is a concept of man; a changeable concept; not conforming to preordained limitations; but a man with an essence. Parts of the primal matter can be ignored and therefore undistinguished and therefore, in a pragmatic sense, non-existent. But one part of the primal matter cannot be ignored. Man is aware of himself. And this awareness is itself an action. But simultaneous with this awareness man necessarily defines himself. As Quine remarks, "To vary Neurath's figure with Wittgenstein's, we may kick away our ladder only after we have climbed it."[29] Sartre sometimes talks as if we can visualize man removed from his actions – temporally prior to situations, problems, awareness. But the process begins in the middle. Experience is the temporal starting point, to paraphrase Kant, but it is not the source. Nor is some given interpretive element the source. Both change in relationship to one another. And change entails freedom. But man is never free in the sense of being totally external to what goes on. God's execution – insofar as it is on intellectual grounds – turns on the impossibility of conceiving this totally external being. Surely Sartre does not wish to resurrect man in God's image.

Plantinga remarks that "For Sartre *every* action, *every* choice, is necessarily right."[30] But this does not do justice to Sartre. It is only true, in a sense. Works of art are not antecedently good or bad. But every painting is not therefore good. Nor is it impossible to have standards. But they are only good or bad once created. Every action *is* right in the sense that there are no external forms in terms of which we may judge it. But actions form framework.

---

[29]   Quine, *op. cit.*, *Word and Object*, p. 4.
[30]   Plantinga, *op. cit.*, p. 248.

And within these frameworks there are values. In this sense an action can be wrong.

It ought not be thought that imposition of the categories and/or the alteration of them are separable or distinguishable mental processes. Imposing and altering categories on the one hand and having experiences – doing things – are two concepts and processes which "live by taking in each other's washing".[31] One does not happen *before* the other. They are processes distinguishable in the nature of things via analysis. The actor acts. And in so acting he creates an image.

We asked earlier "Ought we accept a certain category C?" And we distinguished between different levels of categories, i.e., between *book-tables* and *causality*. But on the Lewis-Sartre position the difference is one of degree. It is more difficult to conceive of an alternative to *causality* because it is a deeply entrenched concept – which means that the concept has a high value. "Every event has a cause" is true. Furthermore, we regard it as necessarily true. But to say it is a necessary truth is not to remark on its intrinsic character but to remark on the community's attitude towards the proposition. But the question "Ought we accept a certain category C?" is of interest. It is closely related to the question "Ought we do *a*?" – when *a*, again, is some action. We can, perhaps, significantly speak of changing the framework by eliminating certain low level concepts, e.g. *book*, *table*, etc. Moreover, it might even make sense to speak of altering or eliminating high level concepts such as *causality*, *time*, etc. But what cannot be made sense of is the elimination of the entire framework in one fell swoop! The sensibility of the ought question travels along a continuum which parallels a continuum on which are placed concepts in accordance with their level or position in the entire framework. Ought questions can significantly be asked about various elements on the concept continuum. But we cannot significantly inquire as to whether we ought to eliminate the entire continuum. Evaluative concepts are on the continuum. Therefore,

[31] J. L. Austin, *Sense and Sensibilia* (Oxford, Clarendon Press, 1962), p. 4. Austin uses this vivid description while discussing the relationship between *sense-data* and *material things*.

evaluative concepts can be altered. But the total elimination of the continuum – or framework – would involve the acceptance of some part of it and hence make logically impossible that activity.

Now consider the question "Ought we do *a*?" – where *a* is some action. Plantinga's objection to Sartre's view can be put in terms of the sensibility of asking this question. On Plantinga's view Sartre makes the question senseless and, therefore, morals or ethics impossible. But *a* – the action – can be described in various ways. Taking the arsenic can be described by "taking the arsenic", "killing yourself", "asking for trouble", "committing suicide", "sinning", etc. Under each of these descriptions the answer to the ought question varies. The question "Ought he have killed his next door neighbor?" might receive a different answer than "Ought he have killed the fellow who raped his wife?" although his next door neighbor *was* the fellow who raped his wife. Now each of these descriptions of *a* is analogous to some concept on the concept continuum. We can meaningfully inquire whether concept C ought be rejected. Likewise, we can meaningfully inquire whether he should have done *a* – *under a description D*. It is not that it is patently obvious what we will say about the action *a* under the description D. (Sartre sometimes makes it seem as if it is.) Likewise, it is not at all obvious how we will answer the ought question about the concept C. What is important, however, is that these questions are meaningful or significant. But it would be a serious conceptual mistake to place on the concept continuum the meta-concept *accepting the entire framework as it is*. This cannot go on the continuum for we cannot significantly challenge its right to be there. Analogously, when we describe *a* as an action which creates man's image we cannot significantly question whether one ought to have done it. Every action can be described as an action which creates man's image. But under this description the ought question is inappropriate. This way of describing *a* must be taken off the description continuum for reasons closely related to the reasons for taking the meta-concept off the concept continuum.

There are descriptions of *a* which allow for the ought question. But there is one description of *a* which doesn't. This is no trivial linguistic point that Sartre is making. He is trying to bring to our attention the fact that human actions are characterizeable in a wide variety of ways one of which is the image creating characterization. If someone's action comes to be viewed this way, and it always can be, it is no longer appropriate to judge it ethically. (Indeed, the whole continuum or framework may *be* overthrown, but we cannot ask whether it ought be.) The art critic makes standard judgments characterizing the work of art as an *R* or an *S*. He properly makes judgments when he is thus describing the work of art. And by each decision he is reinforcing those standards. Suddenly he is confronted with a work of art which does not conform to the standards. But it is good! He says so. His decision cannot be appraised in terms of the old standards. He is not *seeing it as* an instance of this or that sort of art or as conforming to this criterion or that one. He is making a decision viewing the art object as an art object. His decision will perhaps dramatically alter standards. But it cannot be judged in terms of the new ones or the old ones. Indeed, standard decisions – every decision – reinforce standards. But the radical situation depicted dramatically underscores the Sartrian point. It is almost as if the critic cries out to us, "If this cannot be construed as good art then nothing can be!" And there are analogous ethical decisions. It is no easy task to characterize them. Extracting someone's eyes for having blinded another was perhaps, *is* perhaps, characterizeable in ways which allow us to say it is right. But then there is the moment – the time – when we suddenly *see it as* wrong! And the response to the interrogation, "Why ought we not extract his eyes?" is simply "It's wrong!" If the action is *seen as* wrong standards change and future cases can be judged in terms of the new standards. But the initial confrontation of the action outside the standards is not subject to ethical evaluation. I do not wish to suggest that the object of confrontation in the situation where the agent sees an action outside of the standards is formless, i.e. a sort of pure given. I am totally unwilling to countenance a pure given. Also, I would not countenance a pure interpretive. This is an epistemological position which, however, has, for me, serious ethical ramifications. The pure given and the pure interpretive are convenient fictions employed in the process of conceptual analysis.

But they are not confrontable. I should not be taken, therefore, as putting forward some kind of ethical intuitionism if that commits one to the position that on some occasions the object of ethical confrontation is totally uninterpreted. What I am suggesting is that what we can say of a confrontation is a function of how we see it. We always see it as something. The moral action seen as an image-making or essence-making action cannot permit ought questions.

Suppose we distinguish between an action-type and an action token. Action types are analogous to sentences. They are not locatable in space and time. And as statements are to sentences, action tokens are to action types. Statements are instances of sentences. When Jones says "I am here" and Smith says "I am here", they are both making statements, spatially and temporally locatable, which are instances or occurrences of the sentence 'I am here.' Similarly when Jones shoots his great uncle and when Smith shoots his great uncle they are both performing actions of a certain type. Here we could refer to the type as *great uncle shooting* and the actions as Jones shoots *his* great uncle and Smith shoots *his* great uncle. Let T be some ethical action type and $t_1 \ldots t_n$ be token of T. Action tokens are reacted to by the community. If the action tokens are moral then, typically, members of the society evaluate the action. Now it might be supposed that each and every t_i is reacted to in roughly the same way by members of the community. Indeed, if Jones is your best friend you might react differently to his shooting his grandmother than to Smith's shooting – assuming you do not know Smith. But given a similar context – (this would require a great deal of explication) – it might be safely supposed that reactions to t_1 and t_2 will be somewhat alike. This is so because the laws – moral and legal – are always in terms of action types rather than action tokens. Indeed, it would probably be absurd to speak of laws in terms of tokens since they would thereby lack the universality required of laws. This is as true for moral and legal laws as it is for scientific laws. Moreover, I believe for much the same reason, *viz.* the usefulness of the law is totally precluded. But notice that there are sometimes situations where some t_i is reacted to in a significantly different sort of way. We might refer to this kind of reaction as the *that's the last straw attitude*. A long string of action tokens of the type T_s 'teen-age car stealings' are reacted to in a somewhat standard fashion. Then we encounter t_n. But it's the last straw. The guilty party inquires as to why his action token should be reacted to any differently than the action tokens $t_1 \ldots t_n\text{-}1$. And we are hard pressed to answer. We cannot justify our reaction by reference to laws in terms of T_s. We would be dishonest if we redescribed the action t_n so as to justify our reactions in terms of some other law. (Sometimes this is the move but not always!) What we must see is that t_n is being viewed as an essence-making action.

One primary reason for our discussion of Sartre is that a *closely related* phenomenon occurs with non-value events in science. It can suddenly come to pass that a happening is viewed differently than one might expect given that it is an event of a certain type. Along comes e_1 of type E and e_1 gets viewed as a *theory breaker* and/or *creator*. It is not that this cannot be accounted for. But there cannot be a procedure for determining when it will come. Most important, however, is that here again we cannot justify our reactions in terms of prior or future standards which are being broken down or created.

To justify by the standards being changed would be self-contradictory. To justify by the standards emerging would be question begging and non-virtuously circular. Certainly much has been said on this score by philosophers of science, epistemologists, and others.

Mary Warnock remarks that

> ... Sartre seems to be suggesting not only that people do not have functions, as paper-knives do, but that there is nothing *common to* human beings, or *essential* to *human nature*, which may limit their freedom of choice.[32]

In the section of her book in which she discusses Sartre's position Mary Warnock sympathetically attempts to discredit the Sartrian position in a way which strikes me as typical of much contemporary anti-*Sartrian* literature. She makes Sartre out to be a kind

[32]   Mary Warnock, *Ethics Since 1900* (London, Oxford University Press, 1960), p. 166.

of radical ethical intuitionist. She, and others, seem to overlook the fact that existence *precedes* essence. It does not *supplant* it. Essence must exist in order that existence precede it. And the essence that existence precedes is man's essence. Hence, man has an essence.

Unfixed and mutable as it is, it, nonetheless, necessarily exists for Sartre. What Mary Warnock should say is that there is nothing *necessarily* common to human beings, or *necessarily* essential to human nature.

Let me reiterate what I take to be the essential point of these comments by rethinking the issue in terms of ethical justification. In a formal system we deduce consequences by employing logical laws of the system. A formal proof may be viewed as a justification of the last line of that proof. But the laws which permit the movement from premises to conclusion are themselves justifiable. They are justified in terms of the acceptability of the conclusions derivable from them. It can come to pass, however, that a line deduced from premises by use of the laws is viewed in such a way as to have us reject the system. We surely cannot justify our indictment of this conclusion in terms of the system. Indeed, future derivations of lines of the same type might be justified by means of the new system constructed in virtue of our reaction to the line derived but unacceptable in the old system. But we cannot justify in terms of *any* system our discrediting of that particular line. In a similar fashion we justify ethical behavior by an appeal to higher principles. These principles are ultimately justifiable in terms of the behavior they justify. Sartre need not deny this rationalistic attitude toward ethical justification. But what he shows us is that we may confront the ethical action token in such a way as to lead to the reconstruction of the principles. And when the action token is so viewed it cannot be justified. Not every ethical action token is so viewed. Indeed, most are not. But every ethical action token is so viewable! And the sensitive moral agent, recognizing this, realizes that his standard behavior is an implicit affirmation of the standards in terms of which he is behaving. The sensitive moral agent, therefore, can see every moral action in two rather different ways. In only one of these is the action token a possible subject of an ought question. The insensitive agent might see all actions in only one kind of way. But *sometimes* the action token might be seen in just one way, *viz.* as an essence-making action. And, in this case, it cannot be ethically judged. These dramatic cases merely focus on one dimension of every action token. The super-sensitive moral agent who sees all – or nearly all – action tokens as essence making is sacrificed as a martyr, in some sense, for society. He is institutionalized. We cannot judge him. It is not simply that we should not. We cannot! Perhaps this man is the existential man. Perhaps some of us have seen the room whirl, the standard ontological delineations blur and the ethical delineations grow hazy in a closely related manner. Characters in Sartre's literary works undergo this terrifying process. But we pull up short. The room reorients itself – perhaps somewhat differently than it began. The standards return – perhaps radically modified. And then factual and ethical judgment becomes meaningful again.[33] Men may be placed on a sanity continuum. The supersensitive man at one end – mad, but not subject to ethical judgment. On the other end the super-insensitive man – dead, a thing, behaving at all times in accordance with the standards.

Ask yourself what Sartre means by claiming that prior conceptions impose limitations. Our freedom results from there being no prior conception of man – prior to action. But how does a prior conception limit freedom? The prior conception of a paper cutter limits our judgments concerning the specific paper cutter *p-c*. We determine whether it is a good or bad paper cutter based on this prior conception. Still more important we determine whether *p-c* *is* a paper cutter based on a prior conception. Sartre holds that man can come up with prior conceptions of paper cutters. And in a sense he can and does. But (1) it is not necessary that he have such a conception and (2) the concept is not totaly prior to the instances of it. On this statement of Sartre's view the same is true for the concept of man, except that in this case man makes his own concept of *himself*. Papercutters do not make concepts of

---

[33]   One might also view this as a literary metaphor depicting the psychological phenomenon of scientific theorizing.

paper-cutters. Man does the job. Sartre, however, should pay more careful attention to the similarities between these two situations rather than concentrating *almost* exclusively on the dissimilarities. There are no absolutistic conceptions of paper cutters. And there are no absolutistic conceptions of man. Man, in part, determines each. When I say man is, in part, the determiner I do not mean to suggest that he is a part-time determiner. It is not that sometimes he is and sometimes he isn't. Rather every action determines in part, or in a sense.

Finally, to show that I remain a sober analyst, I ask you to consider the following: Relativistic ontological relativism presupposes choice. But couldn't *choice* be another myth? Perhaps. But it is a myth that we must take *quite* seriously since we can choose to disregard it – and in so doing we should have affirmed our belief in it.

We can only make sense of the question, How is the world?, within a framework. The ability to explain things, to predict things, to characterize things, does not eliminate man's freedom. Indeed, it presupposes it. One can, perhaps, try to give the true picture of things independent of a framework or a set of theories. But in so doing he is doomed to failure.

VI

CONCLUDING REMARKS:
HISTORIAN, QUA SUPER-SCIENTIST

The social scientists concern with free will seems to me strangely ironic. His concern is with the freedom of the objects of his study. Yet man's freedom is most strikingly revealed by considering the nature of scientific investigation. The complex task of scientific inquiry which involves redescription, theory construction and, quite often, *reontologizing*, assures man's freedom. The scientific ideal is not *getting things straight* independent of a framework or a set of interrelated theories. This ideal is not simply unattainable; it is unattainable in principle. However, once it is realized that the most reasonable framework to be employed is not totally arbitrary but is likewise not subject to determination by any a priori decision procedure man's freedom of choice is more clearly seen. The ultimate justification for the extreme brand of pragmatism being recommended here is itself pragmatic. But when we understand this we can reasonably say that its acceptability is based on its correctness.

The historian must be a super-scientist because he is constantly shifting back and forth between information gatherer and theory constructor. However, I must confess that my real reason for dubbing the historian a super-scientist is somewhat facetious. It is not so much that *he* is a super-scientist. Moreover, it is not the case that the nature of his study requires that he be a super-scientist. Rather, it is that the deplorable state of the historical inquiry requires that he become or, better yet, recognize that he is a *scientist*. And the job of recognizing this adds to his already complex task and thus requires him to be a super-scientist. The contemporary psychologist and sociologist, determined as they are to be scientific, have often displayed remarkable lack of insight into the nature of scientific inquiry. The historian, on the other hand, sensitive to the peculiar relativism of science, but not rigorously sensitive, has thought that turning history into a science would amount to making something of history which it should not be. This fear is, I believe, ill-founded. An examination of the nature and history of science should reveal this.[1]

I have tried throughout this essay to walk a middle ground. My fear is that both historian *and* philosopher will react negatively because of the compromise. But if my method was imprudent my motives were honorable. For I am deeply concerned with the historical enterprise. My hope is that, in some small way, I should have started the historian down a correct path in order that he might *get things straight*.

[1] See especially Thomas S. Kuhn, *The Structure of Scientific Revolutions* (= *International Encyclopedia of Unified Sciences*, Vol. II, no. 2) (Chicago, The University of Chicago Press, 1962).

EPILOGUE

*The Two New Riddles of Explanation Theory
or The Two Old Riddles of Philosophy of Science**

Philosophical views and positions evolve by writing them down and discussing them. Essays do not emerge, especially from my pen, in a finished form. This remark does not refer simply to syntax (grammatical or logical) but to the substance of the position as well. What seemed to me a semi-defense of Hempel's basic position on explanation now strikes me as a revolutionary alteration of that view. For this reason these remarks are appended.

Let me begin with a highly metaphorical remark. It is a remark which now seems to me extremely platidudinous but nonetheless worth making once in a while. It strikes me that when the grand book of philosophy of science is written, i.e. when that book which characterizes in some detail the correct view on the methodology of science is compiled, the very *final* section should be the true view on explanation and prediction. In fact, given that explaining and predicting are the ultimate ends of scientific and/or explanatory disciplines this final section may not need writing; rather it shall be covered by virtue of the book being completed. It appears that the last twenty five years of writing on explanation theory have mistakenly adopted the opposite position, *viz.* that one must come close to getting things right on explanation and prediction before one can go on to the other problems in the philosophy of science. My position, therefore, is best viewed as an explanation theory sketch which will be filled out when phi-

* I am most grateful to a number of people whose comments on the body of this book has resulted in my getting clearer on what I've been trying to say. I am especially indebted to the members of my Philosophy 47 class at City College of New York for their sympathetic persistence that I make my point of view more conspicuous. I have never learned more in teaching a class than I did with these people.

losophy of science is completed. The overstatement is obvious. However, it seems to me essential to make note of it since it depicts as vividly as possible the important difference in *attitude* between Hempel's view and my own.

The matter of attitude is of some importance. If I am right, the people discussing explanation for the past twenty five years or so have been over conditioned by Hempel's type of question. Certainly there have been antagonists to the model. But my feeling is that *even* they – (*especially* they) – have accepted more than they realize in that they have accepted the Hempelian framework of discussion. This seems amply illustrated by the dispute concerning whether or not laws are implicitly employed in historical explanations. Hempel says they are. Scriven says they aren't. Now what? What has been tacitly accepted is the commitment to the importance of answering this question in some clear way. But is this really an interesting or important question. Hempel's analysis is an analysis of the one place predicate "is an explanation". And, as such, it has certain merits. But it is one thing to insist that an analysis such as Hempel's serve to distinguish between *explanations* and *apples* and quite another to insist that it distinguish between *explanations* and *explanation sketches* or *explanations* and *purported explanations*. When we question the historical explanation as to its satisfactoriness we are really questioning whether or not it is the best that can be given. What turns on whether it passes the a priori minimal conditions for being an explanation? This now strikes me as the worst sort of Aristotelian essentialism. Taxonomy is not without value. In fact, much philosophy is construable as a sort of taxonomical enterprise. And, indeed, some do appear to confuse explanations with apples. But the more interesting question to be considered is what is the correct analysis of the two place predicate "is a better explanation than".[1] And what one says about the analysis of "is an explanation" should be conditioned by the desire to ultimately come up with a correct account of "is a better explanation than".

---

[1] Jack Vickers pointed this out to me five years ago but I just recently saw what he meant. The length of time required was not a function of Vickers' lack of clarity in making the point.

Hempel, in "Aspects", seems guilty of an inconsistency. As I have suggested, some of his arguments against the opponents of the structural identity thesis seems to me incompatible with his own arguments against the sufficiency of his condition of adequacy. The position I have presented restores the structural identity thesis by virtue of upholding the sufficiency of the Hempelian condition of adequacy. Of course this is not the only way out of the inconsistency. Moreover, I have not come to the position because of some a priori belief that the structural identity thesis must be maintained. As a matter of fact I was struck for some time by its *prima facie* implausibility. The actual situation is that the view I am suggesting seems correct on independent grounds. But, as a matter of fact, the structural identity thesis follows from it. Hempel's motivation for denying the sufficiency of the condition of adequacy seems to me to be involved with his preoccupation with the causal account. For Hempel, the question, "Why did E happen?" means something like "What *caused* E to happen?" And, the why question is the paradigm of the scientific question requesting an explanation. But I fail to see what has been added by calling an explanation a *causal* explanation. Hempel does not supply us with an analysis of causality. Indeed, he undermines his own basic predispositions by constantly bringing in examples of non-causal explanations. In the face of the missing analysis of causality and the examples of explanations which are plainly non-causal I would call for an abandonment of the notion of the causal explanation and, in the light of this, a reevaluation of the concept of explanation. And, on my reading, when you throw out the non-explicit commitments which come from his focusing on causal explanation I see that Hempel's own condition of adequacy takes on a far more important role. Hempel might view himself as simply endorsing a Humean position on causality. This is manifest in his requirement of general laws in the explananda which are synthetic. But when Hempel makes this demand is he not really demanding that there be general laws which are *causal*? And then we may inquire as to what he means by a causal law. Far more in keeping with Hume's view – (his focus on mental habits) – is that the explanans of an explanation increase our belief that the event being explained took place and, furthermore, that the explanans be subject to further filling in. Perhaps, on this account, laws will typically appear in explananda. But the crucial questions are 1) Are the laws there because they increase degree of belief or are they there because that's what we must have in order to have an explanation? and 2) What has been added by regarding, either explicitly or implicitly, the laws as causal? My answers, of course, are that the laws need not be there but may be if they serve the functions of increasing degree of belief in the explanandum event and that nothing is added – indeed much is lost – by insisting that the laws be causal. I should almost be willing to go so far as saying that Hempel has misconstrued Hume's view on causality. And what has brought this about? Second rate intellectual psychoanalysis as this might be I must answer the question: It has come about by virtue of a deep seated commitment to the analytic-synthetic distinction. For Hempel, holding on to the analytic-synthetic distinction takes the form of holding on to the notion of the causal explanation. Sweep aside the analytic-synthetic distinction and with it goes the causal explanation. This together with the casting aside of the radical reductionistic methodology manifest in Moore's remarks about *good* and early twentieth century remarks about sense datum leads me to a relativistic position on explanation. The above remarks need a spot of unpacking. The unpacking consists, I'm afraid, of some general remarks. But the nature of the situation calls for generality.

The primary virtue of logical positivism as a philosophical position lay in the fact that the positivists justified obsession with clarity and rigor resulted in a position which, unlike its somewhat obscure predecessor, Berkeleyan and Humean Empiricism, not only contained the seeds of its own destruction but was so clearly stated that these seeds quickly flowered and were thereby observable by even the most naive philosophical onlookers. No group was more aware of these deficiencies than the positivists themselves and, as a matter of fact, much of the early work heading up to the abandonment of the fundamental tenets of the position was done by the positivist planters. It seems, however, that intellectual honesty can only be carried so far and the missionary-like attitude of so many early positivists – (the possessiveness associated with motherhood) – prevented them from seeing the roots and dogmas which had to be abandoned. But the post-positivistic theoreticians, e.g., Quine and Goodman, were able to profit from the perspicuity of the positivistic flaws and framed arguments and positions – (Goodman's on induction and Quine's on the more sweeping topics of language and ontology) – which currently serve as take off points for much contemporary writing.

Quine in "Two Dogmas of Empiricism", and *Word and Object* points out that empiricism has always rested rather uncomfortably on two fundamental dogmas, *viz.* the dogma of the analytic-synthetic cleavage and the dogma of radical reductionism. Likewise, Goodman, in *Fact, Fiction and Forecast*, suggests that the ultimate difficulties in empiricistic, positivistic attempts to "straighten out" the problem of induction – (Hume possibly withstanding) – emerge from a commitment to a form of radical reductionism – (Hume not withstanding).

Quine, in "Two Dogmas of Empiricism", claims that radical reductionism and the analytic-synthetic dichotomy are dogmas which are "at root identical". There is never any attempt made by Quine to show statements of these dogmas to be equivalent in a logical sense. Perhaps the remark is best construed as pointing out a purported psychological fact, *viz.* that those who are predisposed to accept one dogma seem predisposed to accept the other. And with this I can agree. However, there is another sense in which the two dogmas might be construed as equivalent, *viz.* that of being equally fundamental or pervasive and similar in their capacity to lead to mistaken conclusions. And in this sense I do not regard the two D's as equivalent. Radical reductionism strikes me as a more fundamental and positively evil dogma.

The doctrine of *radical reductionism* is not to be confused with the doctrine of *reductionism*. Radical reductionism has, on my view, appeared in three different guises, *viz.* the linguistic, the conceptual and the ontological. The feature common to radical reductionism in all three guises is that there are necessarily certain necessary primitive units. These units will vary depending on the guise. Thus, for linguistic radical reductionism the primitive units are basic terms or sentences; for conceptual radical reductionism the units are certain concepts; for ontological radical reductionism the units are sense-data or physical objects of a certain sort or events of a certain kind. In contrast, reductionism merely claims that reductions or analysis (linguistic, conceptual or physical) can be performed and that what one reduces to is, in some sense, more basic than that which was reduced. But it does not maintain, as did Moore, the radical reductionist, that there are necessarily certain basic necessary units, e.g., "red" (redness), "good" (goodness).

Moore's remarks on definition in the first part of *Principia Ethica* are, perhaps, paradigmatic of the view I refer to as radical reductionism. Here the view comes forth in the domain of ethics where it has had a long and glorious history (cf.: Plato's *Euthyphro*). Moore's work, like the work of the positivists of the '30's, had the affect of first leading people to believe that the true course had finally been discerned but then resulted in people's realizing that all Moore had actually done was to plainly work the error of our ways into ethical analysis by *not so clearly* carrying it to its logical extreme. Moore's position *should* be seen as nothing more than the sense-datum view in ethical clothes. Moreover the sense-datum view is, in actuality, one of the unfortunate mistakes that emerges from the dogma of radical reductionism. Hempel's position on explanation is a more subtle outgrowth of this commitment.

What then, you may justifiably wish to know, is wrong with radical reductionism? And, what is to replace it? See Quine and Goodman is my quick response. They, unlikely as it might seem, are the saviors who have freed us from the bonds of radical reductionism. Though it is distastefully like an author hammering home the moral of his own story I feel this compulsion to make known the very general posture that I have assumed in writing this book.

On my view an explanation is for an agent A under some description D_k in a theory T_k at a time t_n. Moreover, it is an explanation if his belief in the explanandum event is justifiably increased and, furthermore, is susceptible to filling in which would still further justifiably increase the belief in the explanandum event of the agent A under description D_j – (Where j may or may not equal k) – in a theory T_j – (where j may or may not equal k) – at a time t plus n – (where n is greater than O). What goes into the evidence class or explananda of an explanation is conditioned by this criterion. Laws may appear. It might even be shown that they must appear. But this would be so on the basis of the fact that their inclusion is required to satisfy the above condition. The deductive-nomological model strikes me as a bit of a priori taxonomy which has been asked to bear far too great a load. There are no deductive-nomological explanations. But then again there mightn't be any apples which satisfy some roughly accurate a priori criterion laid down for applehood. This would not obviate the usefulness of having a model for appleness. Such is the case with the deductive-nomological model. Also, the remarks made should lead us away from too rigidly focusing on explanations why. Explanations how, what and why should be placed on equal footing. In addition, the analysis suggested by my sketch should reveal the incredible complexity of the explanatory process more conspicuously than Hempel's sketch. Most important, the concentration on the two placed predicate "is a better explanation than" should lead us to answers which are of greater interest to practicing scientists. Parenthetically I must remark that I am struck by the fact that Moore's primary preoccupation with "good" has lead to a sorry situation in the area of ethical analysis. And, related to this, I believe that the working out of a theory of explanation on my terms would tend to blur the distinction between explanation and justification and, thereby, be relevant to problems in ethics. The basic *ethical* question seems to me, what is the best thing to do under the circumstances given these alternatives, i.e. what *decision* should I make? The fundamental question of science might be framed as follows: Under the circumstances how should I *decide* to understand what's going on? Both are decision theoretic questions. Therefore, it should be no surprise that I view decision theory as the most crucial conceptual tool to be employed in working out these matters.

The two new riddles of explanation theory, therefore, are the following:

1) What is the correct analysis of "justifiably increases degree of belief"

and

2) What is the correct analysis of the two place predicate "describes the same event as"?

As is all too obvious my intuitions on both matters are dim. I believe that decision theory holds the answer to (1). But in working out the answer to (1) we should be clarifying what has often been called the riddle of induction. But it is in keeping with my earlier remarks that the ultimate resolution of the problem of explanation must wait on solutions to all problems in the philosophy of science. (2) is, perhaps, an even more difficult question. And, of course, not a totally unrelated question. I remarked earlier that my rather simple minded characterization of "describes the same event as" was curious in that on the analysis this relationship was non-symetrical. This now strikes me as far less of a problem than the fact that on the analysis the relationship *is* transitive. If E_1 describes the same event as E_2 and E_2 describes the same event as E_3 then E_1 describes the same event as E_3. But suppose we are interested in deciding between two explanations of a mental phenomenon one of which is in Freudian terms and the other of which is in physiological terms. Plainly any rational dispute concerning the correct decision must rely on the assumption that both explanations purport to explain the *same* phenomenon. But if the Freudian description of the event, F(D), commits one to certain ontological entities which the physiological description, P(D), does not then it is a bit odd to claim that F(D) describes the same event as P(D) *even if we are willing* to agree that both describe the same event as the ordinary language description of the event, O(D). And one thing – perhaps the only thing – that a theory of explanation should be called upon to do is the following: It should be helpful in deciding which of n competing theories is the more satisfactory by virtue of showing which theory gives better explanations of the *same* events. But before the theory can be helpful in this way we must resolve the matter of the appropriate analysis of "describes the same event as". I do not wish to suggest that the correct analysis of "describes the same event as" should not be transitive. Rather, I wish to point out that the requirement for transitivity reveals the simple-mindedness of my analysis. A more complicated and correct analysis should be able to bear the burden of being transitive. Put it this way: Transitivity is a condition of adequacy that I should impose on the relationship "describes the same event as". My analysis satisfies this condition. But it also inclines one to give up the requirement of this condition. Therefore, one must either have arguments in support of dropping the condition or must have arguments to show that the analysis oughtn't incline you to drop the condition or must have a new analysis. I lack all three. However, I should opt for the last option.

So the new riddles of explanation theory turn out to be very old riddles in the philosophy of science. And I suppose all I ultimately have to say is that I'm just a bit shocked that this wasn't more plainly recognized from the very outset.

FE
N
I
A
M